Butterworth Architecture Management Guides

Quality Management for Building Design

Tim Cornick is a qualified architect with many years of design practice experience. He is currently a Lecturer in Construction Management at the University of Reading, researching and teaching in the areas of quality management for construction and computer-integrated construction. He belongs to national and international working groups and holds a number of research grant awards in his subject areas, and serves on the Royal Institute of British Architects Sound Practice Committee, which provides the architectural profession with guidance on the implementation of quality management.

Butterworth Architecture Management Guides

Quality Management for Building Design

TIM CORNICK, DipArch, RIBA

Butterworth Architecture

Butterworth Architecture
An imprint of Butterworth–Heinemann Ltd
Westbury House, Bury Street, Guildford, Surrey GU2 5BH

 PART OF REED INTERNATIONAL P.L.C.

OXFORD   LONDON   GUILDFORD   BOSTON
MUNICH   NEW DELHI   SINGAPORE   SYDNEY
TOKYO   TORONTO   WELLINGTON

First published 1991

British Library Cataloguing in Publication Data

Cornick, Tim
Quality management for building design – (Butterworth architecture
management guide).
1. Buildings. Design & construction
I. Title
721

ISBN 0–7506–1225–8

Library of Congress Cataloging-in-Publication Data

Quality management for building design/Tim Cornick.
    p.   cm. – (Butterworth Architecture management guides)
Includes bibliographical references and index.
ISBN 0–7506–1225–8
1. Building—Quality control.   I. Title.   II. Series.
TH439.C67   1990
692–dc20   90–47836

Photoset by TecSet Ltd, Wallington, Surrey
Printed and bound in Great Britain by Courier International Ltd.,
Tiptree, Essex

Contents

Contents

Contents

Foreword

In recent years we have seen a welcome improvement in the management of UK construction projects. The speed of building on some sites has shown that, at its best, the UK contracting industry can stand comparison with leading companies in the USA and elsewhere. No less encouraging has been the parallel interest in improving quality standards. Quality Assurance in components and manufactured products is now accompanied by sector schemes covering steel reinforcement and ready-mixed concrete.

The focus of attention is now turning towards the design process. Recent studies have shown that some 50% of defects in building arise through decisions or actions in the design stages. With the costs in Europe of rectifying building failures running at 12–15% of total construction expenditure the rewards for improving quality in design are very great.

The idea of introducing formal quality management into building design is not universally welcomed. Critics claim that procedures will bring a new layer of bureaucratic controls in their wake, which will be expensive, time consuming and – perhaps most worrying – stifle the creativity and independence of the design professional.

However, early experiences are already showing that these concerns are largely unjustified. Of course, good design management involves an inescapable reliance on procedures, but there is no evidence that, once in place, observance of these systems puts an undue burden on the design teams. Indeed, a properly considered framework for action can help the participants to perform effectively, with far less time devoted to troubleshooting, corrections, and chasing information that should have been readily available in the first place.

The idea that creative design may be inhibited is equally erroneous. Certainly, innovative ideas will be tested in a well-ordered system, but that is as it should be. Practising designers know that the conceptual design process still depends on a properly considered brief, and thereafter the design process calls increasingly for consultation, the prepararation and exchange of technical information and the coordination of a large number of specialist inputs.

This book, which lays down a fundamental model for design process control and draws on the practical experience of the PSA and other leading design practices, provides a valuable insight into the correct approaches needed and the benefits that can be achieved with the introduction of effective quality management in building design.

Bryan Jefferson
Director General of Design, PSA
October 1989

Introduction

Quality is the attainment of a desired level of excellence which has been clearly defined in terms of requirements for the people, processes and finished product of the client's building. It is *not* achieved through mountains of paperwork of manuals, checklists, etc., which may all take extra time and money. It *is* achieved by committed, trained and knowledgeable people in the design practices, construction companies and client organizations involved in the building project, who:

○   Agree their *requirements* throughout every phase of the project.

○   Use simple but clear methods of *communication* from the giving of the initial brief all the way through to giving a specific instruction on-site.

○   Believe that it *is* really possible to get things right first time, every time throughout the complex processes of the total building project.

○   Carefully plan to ensure that they actually *prevent* things going wrong in the first place.

○   Use personnel and documented systems of control that need the *absolute minimum* of bureaucracy to achieve the desired result.

○   Openly admit that change, for whatever reason, is always likely and *honestly* control it.

Quality management is systematic process control throughout every phase of the building project, and quality assurance is the result for both supplier and customer alike. If its principles are properly understood and applied by *all* the people involved in the project, the end result can only be a reduction in cost, because wasted time and resources have been avoided, and a raising of standards, because repairs and rework will not occur. *Everyone* must play their part, including the client, in making the necessary cultural change in attitude. Clients must accept that they are part of the building production process and clearly define their requirements; designers must ensure they have interpreted those requirements and clearly specify the requirements for the building; and contractors must fully accept that the requirements are achievable.

If the construction industry and its clients get quality management right it will save *millions*!

The basis of this book

This book is the result of a research project funded by the Science and Engineering Research Council and carried out in the Department of Construction Management, University of Reading. The project set out to develop a quality management model for building products that would embody the principles of quality and apply them to established processes. This model would be the means of effecting continuous improvement in the corporate managements of the different companies, practices and organizations that contributed to the building project.

This research was carried out by the author in conjunction with two Research Fellows, each of whom contributed their experience, knowledge, enthusiasm and commitment to the work and without whom this book would not have been possible. Reg Grover is an architect and building technology consultant who is currently guiding a leading UK architectural practice into implementing its own quality management system. John Broomfield is a quality consultant and currently a director of Quality Management International, with the responsibility for directing the work of his consultancy in supporting construction companies and architectural and engineering practices to correctly implement their own quality management system.

It is the sincere hope of all three that this book will help clients, consultants and construction companies to get quality assurance and management 'right first time', as there is evidence that they are not! If the principles of quality management are correctly applied to building projects – and the client, design and construction organizations that produce them – then the result will be the raising of standards and the reduction of costs. If these principles are not fully understood and misapplied then the result could well be the opposite!

This book concentrates in detail on the design contribution to the building project, as it is in this particular area that the client's needs and expectations have to be determined and interpreted for construction. Chapters 1–5 deal with the construction industry's and its clients' concern for improved quality, the fundamental philosophy and mechanisms of quality management as they have been generally defined and understood in other fields and what the implications are of applying these principles to the work of the building designer. Chapter 6 describes the model in terms of its phase and task division, its element types of inputs to the tasks that are of concern to project management and finally its detail types of input to each of the elements that are of concern to corporate management. Chapters 7–10 describe in detail how the model is applied to those phases of the building project that are of prime concern to the building designer. They also suggest what aspects of the Quality System Standard are particularly relevant to each of these phases, what the designers' role is in each situation and the specific problems that need to be solved to achieve quality improvement in the design process. Chapter 11 deals with the designer's role in those phases of the project which are not his prime concern and Chapter 12 sets out the requirements for the successful application of quality management to building design. A series of short case studies of early examples of the practical application of quality management to building design practice ends the book.

Finally, the author would like to acknowledge the support of Professor Bill Biggs, particularly with the original research project and generally with teaching the author (sometimes very painfully!) in his early academic career how to convert from communicating by drawing as an architect to communicating by writing as a lecturer in construction management.

Chapter 1

Quality Assurance and management in building design

The concern for Quality Assurance (QA) and management in building in the UK has a number of different origins. In 1983 the UK, through the initiative of the Department of Trade and Industry, launched a National Quality Campaign for business and industry[1]. This was in order to ensure its future competitiveness in the world markets in terms of improving exports for the obvious benefits in the balance of trade that this should bring and maintain. It was decided that the principles of quality, as practised for many years by, most notably, the Japanese, should be studied and applied to UK industry through an intensive education programme. Financial support for consultancy services to aid companies in setting up quality management systems would also be provided by the government as an additional encouragement.

It was also decided that as the construction industry was an important part of the manufacturing industries as a whole (in that it both used their products and provided their facilities) the quality campaign should also be directed at them. In order to encourage the construction industry to take the application of quality management systems seriously a study of its implications for application to civil engineering was carried out by the Construction Industry Research and Information Association[2].

The result of this early interest by the construction industry in QA was that a number of component manufacturers[3] and large construction companies[4] have implemented quality management systems up to a standard that gives them certification against the British Standard for Quality Systems BS 5750[5], standard which is now internationally harmonized and which carries the joint designation of ISO 9000.

The construction industry also has its own motives for taking the subject seriously. One essential reason was that QA – almost by definition – appears to offer a way of reducing mistakes in the design and construction processes of building which result in costly defects that have to be put right in maintenance. This was of particular concern to the Property Services Agency (PSA), which has the responsibility for design, construction and maintenance of the UK government's building stock. Their own efforts were based on the premise that, as the cause of building defects had been nationally identified as primarily being in the design and construction process, rather than in building products[6], all design consultants and construction contractors should, in the future, be 'quality assured' if they are to take part in government building projects (Fig. 1.1).

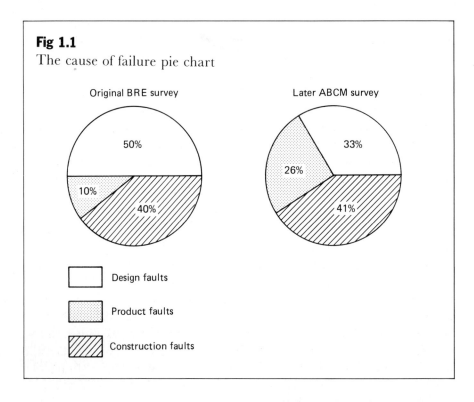

Fig 1.1
The cause of failure pie chart

Original BRE survey

Later ABCM survey

Design faults

Product faults

Construction faults

As an experiment, the PSA's Design Standards Office implemented a quality management system for its own multi-disciplinary design practice and obtained certification to BS 5750[7]. There is also growing evidence that public clients – who still comprise a large proportion of the UK construction market – through both direct government buying departments and local authorities might require QA for their building projects as an extension of their own tests.

Private clients do not have the same sort of political motive as public clients for demanding QA for their building projects and the consultants and contractors who contribute to them. They are concerned that they receive value for money, and that their requirements are fully met. Therefore they seek reassurance that this is possible before appointments are made and guarantees after the project has been completed. This is of particular concern to the type of client who leases or sells the building to another end user.

In an effort to improve the procurement of design and construction services for its members the British Property Federation's system[8] requires a building project to be managed in a more integrated way, and one in which the traditional adversarial contractual arrangements between designer and constructor are overcome by clearly defined roles and responsibilities. This system is, in effect, a formal management system for a building project and, as such, anticipates some of the elements of a quality plan for a project that would be required by a quality management system.

Private clients are, however, still very reluctant to directly demand QA of its consultants and contractors, because they fear, with some justification, that if they do so, QA will be viewed as an extra, and will be charged as an additional cost of the project. The view that QA can somehow be considered as an option for clients to have (or not to have) on their projects has been inadvertently given in a recent publication[9]. Therefore, while the private clients would not wish to discourage any member of the construction industry from implementing QA in their own companies and practices, they have no wish to pay for the improved design and construction service that would result.

The motives for a number of major construction companies introducing QA into their organizations have been somewhat mixed. There has been fear that, unless they do so, they may be excluded from tender lists in the future, especially those of public clients. There has been hope that their public display of 'certified QA' will give them a market edge in the future, even perhaps in the forthcoming single European market, although this hope is by no means yet justified by any of the construction-related directives from the European Commission. Finally, there is a growing realization by some companies that a quality management system, when fully implemented, will not only raise their standards but also reduce their costs and hence increase their profits.

With the construction industry's designers (architects, structural, services and civil engineers) the motives and views are again different and even contradictory. Some architectural practices (with the support of the Royal Institute of British Architects[10]) see the application of a formal quality management system as a means of improving the professional service they give to their clients through an agreed method of standard good practice. Another major factor is that, because the application of a formal quality management system will demand a clear definition of requirements and documented evidence of design and construction processes, design risk can be more readily assessed and the future design liability risk to architectural practice can be reduced[11]. On the other hand, the leading UK multi-disciplinary engineering practice feels that the introduction of QA can add nothing to an already highly regarded professional engineering design consultancy service[12].

Indeed, it is quite a problem for *any* type of professional practice – whether building design or otherwise – to outwardly profess that they are now 'quality assured', as this raises questions about their prior professionalism. There may even be some question as to whether a quality assurance claim may even *increase* the liability of the design professional because a higher 'duty of care' is now expected. However, there is now evidence from the USA that for at least one of the design professions (the civil engineers) a very detailed and formal quality management system *is* becoming the accepted method[13].

A study of what the UK construction industry might be like by the end of the 1990s does, however, recommend that the industry as a whole should apply 'total quality management' to better-integrated design and construction processes using quality assured products. QA could well become mandatory and the norm for building projects, and could change the attitudes of all involved in a project[14].

Problems in modern building design

Evidence suggests that many 'quality-related events' in the construction process are the result of poor communication in the design process[15]. This research, which has been supported by a small local survey[16], points to the fact that errors leading to defects are mostly a result of failing to clearly communicate design requirements to the construction process. The fact that buildings are unique and sometimes innovative projects is *not* the fundamental cause, which is so often why the construction industry thinks problems occur. Defects in finished buildings (which are manifested in various degrees of damage, from the irritating to the disastrous) also seem to be the result of a failure to communicate within the design process technological factors that have been known for many years (e.g. the causes of condensation)[17].

The problems caused in modern buildings therefore seem much more due to deficiencies in managing communication during the design process than to merely technological factors. The resulting building failure is seen to be unacceptable in terms of the amount of money that has to be spent on repairs and maintenance. Increasing liability pressure on the designers (mainly the architects) is not the best answer to the financial problems caused due to the lengthy and not always successful litigation involved. Insuring the project as a whole through single project insurance offers a better means for the client to recover costs quickly, and QA – if it can show that all requirements have been met – may offer a way of assuring insurance companies to support this approach[18].

Managing quality in the briefing and designing phases

The need to manage quality in the briefing, designing and specification phases of a building project, rather than trying to merely control quality in the construction phase, stems from the proposition that prevention is better than the cure. The latter approach will only solve the problems that come to light during construction and not those that remain latent, appearing during the life of the building.

Logically, the requirements for a building can only begin during the *briefing* phase of a project, be further developed during the *scheme* and *detail* design phases, and be finally refined for the physical production of the building during the *specifying* phases. The subsequent *tendering* and *constructing* phases should add nothing to the fundamental requirements of the building's design, as they are concerned only with pricing and controlling the resources necessary to achieve its physical realization.

The management of the processes involved in those four early project phases is therefore vital if the likely causes of quality problems are to be identified and prevented. This is the only cost-effective way that quality can be achieved in the later *constructing* and *maintaining* phases of a building project.

Why design practices should implement quality management systems

There are a number of possible incentives for the design practice – which has the ultimate responsibility for the briefing, designing and specifying phases of a project – to apply a quality management system to its own processes. *Reduced liability risk* is currently most attractive to architectural and engineering practices because of the reduction in professional indemnity insurance premiums. The reason the application of a quality management system may help in this area is because of the systematic discipline that it demands of any process. Such a discipline would essentially ensure that:

○   The requirements that the architect or engineer has been asked to fulfil are clearly defined and agreement that they have been met is recorded.

○   The sources of information that support any design decision making are clearly defined and fully documented.

○   The responsibilities between the architect or engineer and all the other project participants for achieving *total* quality in the project will be clearly defined and demonstrated.

If a quality management system is being applied to a building project it will, by definition, demand that those who construct are, in turn, responsible for meeting their requirements. This will therefore remove from the architect or engineer the difficult and onerous duty of supervision, which carries with it an additional liability. (However, a very positive role for the designer does emerge in the constructing phase of the building project and this is discussed in detail in Chapter 11.)

Increased market share may be another benefit that the architectural or engineering practice may enjoy by implementing a quality management system. This could be because the system itself will lay the foundations of raising standards through continuous improvement in the design service and product that the practice offers to the client. This would also make the practice attractive to other project participants with whom it might be selected to work in a situation where an architect or engineer may not necessarily be the first participant on a building project.

Reducing costs and increasing profits for the architectural or engineering practice 'as a business' has been one of the most powerful incentives for companies outside the construction industry to implement quality management systems. The fact that the approach of doing things right first time, every time is both encouraged philosophically and supported procedurally by the application of a quality management system means that costs must ultimately be reduced. This is self-evident, as *not* doing so must inevitably incur extra costs because work has to be carried out again. The evidence of how costly this waste of human and material resources really is in other industries has been set at 40–60% of turnover, depending on whether a product or service is being provided, and this figure is considered to be no less in any sector of the construction industry. Although this waste can be seen far more readily on the construction site itself, in many cases the causes can be traced back to the design and specification processes, which themselves have been wasteful because revised documentation has been required.

Costing the benefit and effectiveness of implementing a quality management system in a design practice or a construction company is complex. This is partly due to a lack of understanding of how 'prevention', 'appraisal' and 'failure' costs can be identified and related in any organization that deals essentially in projects and partly to the fact that, traditionally, waste of all kinds is priced for in the building procurement process[19].

Only when the architectural or engineering practice examines its own current cost of waste does costing become a powerful incentive. One study currently underway with a company provides the client with a design-and-build service in support of its own implementation of quality management system, and it is expected to take some time before such costs can be clearly identified[20].

Current arguments against quality management systems

These can be summarized in the following statements that are most frequently heard from construction companies and architectural and engineering practices:

o   'Quality is another piece of paperwork . . .'
o   'Quality is being used as a stick to beat the sub-contractors with . . .'
o   Even when we get the quality right we still get beaten on price . . .'
o   Formal QA systems will stifle creative architectural and engineering design . . .'

The first three quotations sum up what the sub-contractors (who find themselves at the end of the chain of responsibility in a building project) feel about the current attempt to apply QA to building[21]. The last is the feeling expressed by a number of architects and engineers. The reasons for the confusion are probably as follows:

o   The industry's traditional experience of QA is with major projects where safety has been a major factor (i.e. offshore, petrochemical and nuclear projects), and in these situations QA has comprised extensive paperwork checking procedures (although it has not necessarily resulted in cost-effective quality management).

o   The Standard that describes the elements of a quality management system (ISO 9000/BS 5750) was written with the manufacturing industries in mind, and consequently most people in the construction industry find it difficult to relate to some of the concepts and language it contains.

o   The confusion may be further compounded by the fact that the Standard applies to a situation where both the design and production processes for a product come under a single and continuous responsibility. This situation is not generally the case in the construction industry, when the product in question is a building. Those who design the product have become separated from those who produce it, the former being the professional architects and engineers and the latter, commercial contractors.

O   The industry probably feels that its traditional rather *ad-hoc* way of going about its business has served it well for many centuries, and that the imposition of any formal quality management systems to its processes would only stifle its creative design, limit its flexibility of response to widely diverse and unique projects and not necessarily result in a perceived improvement in building quality.

Therefore, the confusion that the construction industry has about the subject can be, at best, a genuine misunderstanding of the philosophy and mechanisms of quality management and, at worst, a smokescreen in order to resist change because of an erroneous self-image that it is efficient in its current methods. However, this confusion about quality management systems and current industry practice can be dispelled by answering each of these questions in turn:

1. *'Quality is another piece of paperwork.'* Paper already abounds in the building process and often to no good end. Drawings lack critical information, can be difficult to comprehend by people on-site, and may not coordinate with other documents. Specifications are not specific to the project, contain unachievable requirements and, more often than not, end up being ignored. Bills are shopping lists that are wrong because they only crudely measure the material content of a design. Variation orders and site instructions occur because the production planning requirements of the design have not been thought through in the first place. Management of a project demands some paper in order to transmit the requirements of one participant from another in a clearly defined and recordable way. A quality management system demands only *enough* paper to demonstrate what the requirements are and that they have been met.

2. *'Quality is being used as a stick to beat the sub-contractor with.'* In the building process a chain of conformance to requirements must occur if total quality is to be achieved (see Chapter 6). In practice, the chain relates to a chain of responsibility extending down from client to designer, from designer to general/management contractor, and finally to specialist sub-/trade contractor. The specialist contractor (whether sub- or trade) unfortunately finds himself at the end of that line and is the final downline participant (Fig. 1.2).

The tendency for any upline participant to use QA *against* any downline participant in a negative way can only be attributed to either ignorance or a means of self-protection on the part of the participants

Fig 1.2
The chain of responsibility

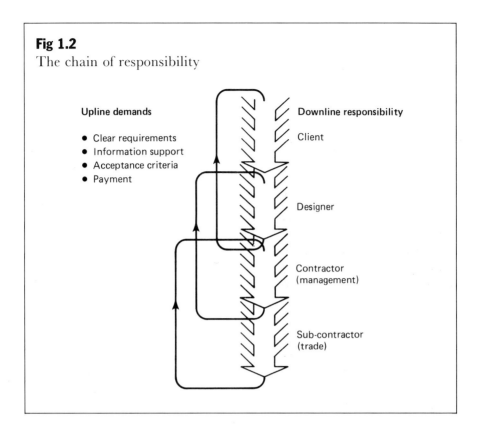

Upline demands

- Clear requirements
- Information support
- Acceptance criteria
- Payment

Downline responsibility

Client

Designer

Contractor
(management)

Sub-contractor
(trade)

upline, because a project quality management system makes as many management demands of the upline participant by the downline participant as the converse. In other industries and companies the key to success in implementing cost-effective quality management has been the recognition of the customer–supplier relationship within and between different processes. In the building process this means that any downline participant is also the customer of any upline participant who should supply: (a) clearly defined and achievable requirements, (b) project information and management support, (c) agreed acceptance critieria for their work and (d) payment for completed work. Therefore if a quality management system is to be used as a stick it can be used as much *by* the downline participant as *against* him! (However, the stick motive should rapidly disappear as soon as all participants are realizing their own benefits by working in this way.)

2. '*Even when we get the quality right, we still get beaten on price.*' For any downline participant a project quality management system means that he can require of the upline participant that the time and technical

performance standard requirements are: (a) clearly defined, (b) achievable with agreed acceptance criteria and (c) appropriately communicated *before* he submits a design or general management fee or specialist construction tender bid. Then if he is beaten on price it will not be at the expense of quality, as this will be achieved by a more cost-efficient competitor.

4. '*Formal QA systems will stifle creative architectural and engineering design . . .*'. Traditional and current theoretical models of how building designers process their thoughts suggest the possibilities shown in Fig. 1.3[22, 23]. In either model it is the 'synthesis' or 'conjecture' function of the thought process that contains any creative element.

A formal quality management system applied to any aspect of architectural or engineering design will neither address nor affect this particular function. A quality management system can only (and will) affect the 'analysis–evaluation' or reasons for the 'refutation' functions of that process by requiring that they be made more explicit. Recent studies suggest that explicit analysis and evaluation is not the normal situation in current architectural practice[24], but formal quality management would require this situation to change.

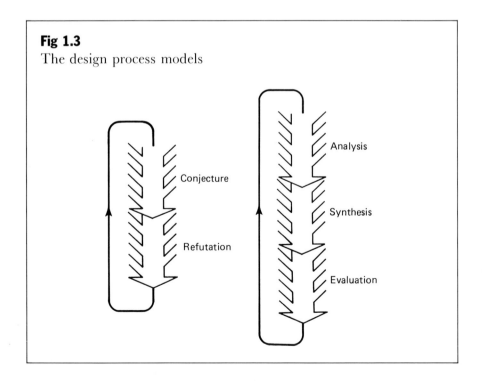

Fig 1.3
The design process models

However, even after dealing with these arguments and demonstrating why they are ill-founded, the reader may still wish to be convinced of exactly how a quality management system will impact on the process of building design itself. This is dealt with first by explaining the generally accepted principles of quality – both its philosophy and mechanisms – and their meaning for building projects, and second by describing a model that embodies those principles and applies them throughout the building project, especially to the phases for which the designer has a prime responsibility.

Chapter 2

Defining quality

If something cannot be defined it cannot be managed. The problem with the word 'quality' is that in particular situations it can have different meanings for different people. The varying interpretations can be exploited for individual ends and – if commercial, professional and legal issues are at stake – can result in costly and time-consuming arguments. The problem of definition is well summarized as follows[1]:

Quality is like politics, or sex, or religion. It is something everyone understands, and is convinced that he does correctly. Few would like to explain it, and discussions on it are generally short and superficial, with one or other of the participants soon changing the subject through boredom or embarrassment. We all think we understand the subject, and are all convinced that our ways are right.

It is worth making the following observations from this quotation that have particular relevance to the process of building design:

O   There are many individual people involved throughout the design and subsequent construction and operation processes of a building project, and everyone's understanding could be subjectively different.

O   The designer has to translate the needs of the client in such a way that they can be realized by the manager and specialist contractors[25], and each participant could change the definition either deliberately or unwittingly.

O   Nearly all traditional disputes that occur throughout the design, construction and operating processes of a building project stem from the fact that each participating individual thought that his or her particular way was right.

In many ways the problem of defining 'quality' is more acute in the building process than in any other production field. This is essentially because the total responsibility for the creation of a building project is divided between many different people and organizations (which may only work together once on any particular project) and, for major works, extends over a comparatively long period of time. Therefore there is a danger that the meaning of quality for any specific aspect of the project can easily become changed over time and distance and between different methods of working. (Communication problems have been cited as the fundamental cause of many of the quality-related events that occur in modern building[15, 16].)

The fact that the client has an implicit expectation of quality for his building, the designers have their own professional view of quality depending on architectural and engineering tradition, and the management and specialist contractors and component manufacturers have to make commercial judgements about quality related to price – all this serves to create confusion over concepts of quality. The organizations who stipulate codes and regulations also impact on the project with their own general collective view of quality, which may itself conflict with those of other participants.

The result of all this confusion over what is meant by 'quality' is so often a dissatisfied client, a disillusioned and sometimes sued designer, commercially embarrassed contractors and distrusted component manufacturers at the end of the design and construction phases of a building project. What then follows is totally unexpected and unwanted maintenance throughout the subsequent operation phase of the project and life of the building.

As it is only through managing the combined outputs of all these different participants that a modern building can occur at all, it follows that the quality aspect of that building – from inception to completion – must be capable of being managed if the result is to be satisfactory. The meaning of 'quality' therefore has to be agreed for the sake of all participants who take part in a project if they are *all* to be successful, especially the designers, who play the key role of being the translators of 'need' into the 'physical reality' of a building (see Fig. 2.1).

Generally accepted definitions

Standard definitions of quality can be derived from two sources and, of the three definitions that emerge, only one is capable of being managed. From the dictionary definitions of 'quality' the notion of some *level of excellence* can be seen to arise. This is the definition that most people feel

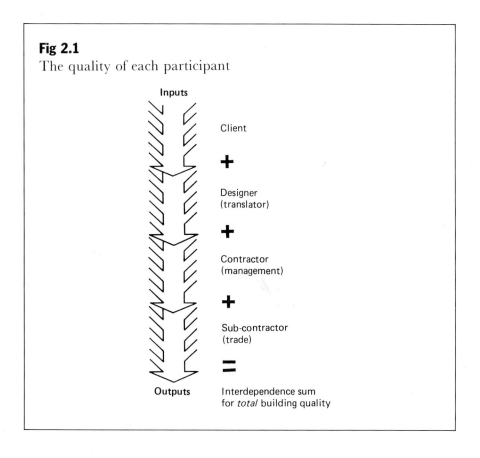

Fig 2.1
The quality of each participant

Inputs

Client

+

Designer
(translator)

+

Contractor
(management)

+

Sub-contractor
(trade)

=

Outputs

Interdependence sum
for *total* building quality

comfortable with – essentially because they can make it mean anything they wish! With regard to building, 'aesthetic' quality is something that is highly subjective and is prone to change from time to time, as does any activity concerned with visual appearance, from product design to fine art.

Even 'excellence' in technical performance can be subjective, as individual people react differently, both emotionally and physically, to the same environment. General expectations (and the codes and standards that reflect those) are constantly changing as a result of social and economic development. Therefore this is a definition that is unacceptable if common agreement is to be reached by all participants for the management of a building project's design and construction.

The next two definitions of quality can be derived from the one found in the British, European and International Standard for Quality Systems[5], which describes 'quality' as 'the totality of features required by a product or service to satisfy a given need'. From this, the following two simple definitions can be derived. Quality is either

o Fitness for purpose; or
o Conformance to (or meeting) requirements.

The first definition has the same appeal as the dictionary's definition because it can also mean what one wishes it to. It can be expected by the customer of any product or service (both of which are to be found in the total building project process) or claimed by the supplier as long as either party can prove it! The problem with this definition is that it requires a further definition of what exactly is the 'purpose' and how 'fitness' can be assessed. This concept poses particular problems in building design, where many spaces and elements are multi-purposed, and a greater fitness for one purpose can only be achieved at a lesser fitness for another, given the cost and time available.

The only definition which is capable of management is that of *conformance to or meeting requirements*. The fact that quality seems to be reduced to something that means nothing more than 'meeting requirements' must come as a disappointment to many people. Indeed, it does to many building design professionals, who would much rather accept the 'level of excellence' version, because this can be endlessly debated. This definition may also seem unacceptable to the ultimate customer in the process – the building client – because he would prefer the 'fitness for purpose' which he would rightly expect in his finished building.

Therefore, to allay those people's fears the hierarchy of these three meanings is suggested in Fig. 2.2 as a means of solving the semantic problem. It can be seen that both a level of excellence and a fitness for purpose can still be achieved from a basis of conformance to requirements – which itself is the only definition that can be successfully managed. This is because requirements are capable of being

o clearly defined by number, text, drawing or example,
o communicated by a variety of media to suit the recipient, and
o reasonably objectively assessed for conformance

regardless of whatever product or service is being offered in any field of human activity. Therefore 'conformance to requirements' can be accepted as the management definition of 'quality'. This must equally apply in building design and all other functions and activities to which it has to relate.

Applying the definition of quality to building design

What does this definition of quality mean in the processes involved in the briefing, designing, specifying and constructing phases of a modern building?

Fig 2.2

Meanings of quality

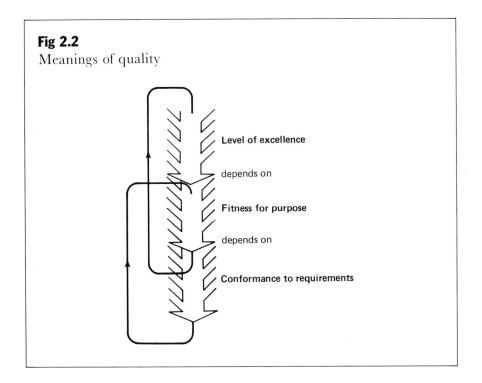

Level of excellence

depends on

Fitness for purpose

depends on

Conformance to requirements

○   The definition of requirements by any upline participant must be in terms that can be reasonably met by another downline participant (see Fig. 1.2).

○   The methods of communication of requirements used by any participant must enable another participant to understand if they can be or have been met.

○   The acceptance criteria for requirements are such that a reasonably objective assessment for conformance can be made.

As the designing phase comes between the briefing and constructing phases, it consists essentially of translating requirements from a developed idea for a building to its physical reality. If there is to be total conformance to requirements set out in the original briefing process (and hence 'quality' for the client) then the 'translating' function of design must successfully deal with the above key issues of definition, communication and acceptance criteria.

In Chapter 1 it was noted that analysis, synthesis and evaluation are the three distinct functions that form a total and iterative design process. If conformance to requirements is the definition of quality, then the achievement of quality is dependent upon:

○   the definition and acceptance criteria being *completely* derived in analysis;

○ the communication being *consistently* maintained from analysis to synthesis, synthesis to evaluation, and evaluation back to analysis;
○ the acceptance criteria being the *only* basis for evaluation.

This should always occur during any design phase of a project. How the definition of quality relates to the design process is shown in Fig. 2.3. The figure shows that, if conformance to requirements is to be the accepted definition of quality, building design practice must allow for rigorous analysis/evaluation functions. Also, the input to and output from the synthesis function (which can still be as individually creative as the particular architect or engineer can make it) must ensure that methods of communication demonstrate requirements and whether or not they have been met.

Fig 2.3

Relating quality to the design process

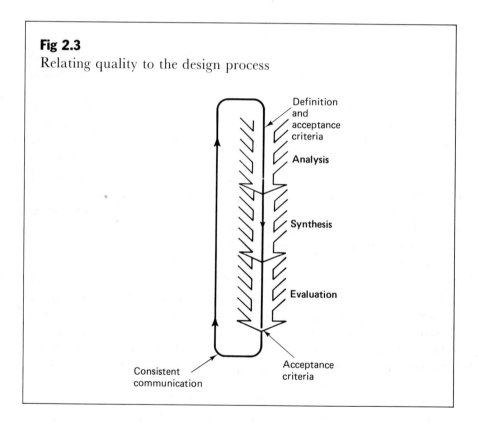

Chapter 3

Quality management, assurance and control

Confusion reigns over the variety of terms being applied to quality and the bureaucracy surrounding the subject, so it is worth clarifying matters at this point.

'Quality Assurance' (QA) is the term most commonly employed by a number of organizations promoting its use[6, 9], and is one that the construction industry relates to the experience of major defence, nuclear and petrochemical projects, where safety is pre-eminent. In this context, QA comprises extensive checking and verification procedures over and above the general design and construction contract requirements. This generates the view that quality means additional bureaucratic procedures, an increase in work and extra cost.

Another term, 'Quality Control', creates images of factory production (and therefore not particularly relevant to the design and construction of buildings) which was where 'quality', and the systems to control it, had its historical roots. To ensure that the 'bullets would fit the barrels' in the field, systematic inspection of the manufactured product had to be introduced. This now somewhat outdated method of controlling quality in the manufacturing industries (i.e. by inspection and rejection of the product) is exactly what happens in the current practice of designing and constructing buildings.

Finally, talk of 'Quality Management' raises the question that surely management of the process exists in any case. How, then, is quality management different? In fact it is not very different, as the formal management system required to be documented could be considered as 'good management, only written down'.

The meanings of the terms

It is not the intention here to quote the official definitions of 'management', 'assurance' and 'control' to be found in the Quality System Standard[5]. A simple comparison of the meanings and relationships of these terms is a better approach to removing confusion in the reader's mind, and this can be done as follows[26]:

Quality is *conformance to requirements*, which is attained through *management for improvement* by all project participants, and this should result in *assurance by demonstration*. Through every phase of a project there are 'customers' who have *requirements* and 'suppliers' who have to *conform* to those requirements, but the ultimate customer is the *client* and the supplier is the *project team*.

In other words:
○   The aim is *quality*, which is defined as conformance to requirements.
○   The method is *management*, which allows for improvement so that non-conformance to requirements can be corrected.
○   The result is *assurance* by demonstration that conformance to requirements has occurred.
○   The mechanism is *control*, which ensures that improvement and assurance can always occur.

Therefore what a quality management system demands of any process (including design) is that its system of control can ensure that conformance to requirements can be 'assured by demonstration' and non-conformance can be corrected through 'management for improvement'. The latter objective is achieved by methods of 'audit', 'review' and 'feedback', all of which will be described in Chapter 5.

Changes required in current building design practice

The changes required in design practice for the implementation of a formal quality management system that results in quality assurance through quality control are not necessarily major ones. The mistake that most people (and the organizations to which they belong) make is to assume that a quality management system is something additional to what they already do. This is not so, but it may require some adjustment to existing practices to ensure that improvement and assurance and the necessary control required can take place.

At this point the reader may even like to remove the word 'quality', as what we are essentially concerned with is really 'process control' – a conclusion that one large client organization reached after embarking on a 'quality improvement mission'[27].

The differences to current design practice may be as follows:

○   The activity of design itself would need greater control as it passes through various phases.

○   A greater number of checkpoints may be required so that proof of conformance can be continually demonstrated.

○   Change – for either the satisfaction of new requirements or correction to ensure that the existing requirements are being met – should be accepted as a positive action and systematically controlled.

None of the above should impact adversely upon the creativity of design, as these differences will still only affect the analysis/evaluation function rather than the synthesis function of the design process. It may mean that less time can be spent on the latter as more has to be spent on the former, but even this problem could be overcome by a greater application of information technology to the analysis/evaluation function of building design[28].

Chapter 4

The fundamentals of quality

The fundamentals of quality were defined by Crosby[29] and interpreted by Mortiboys[1] for the UK Department of Trade and Industry's 1983 National Quality Campaign, and were proposed as follows

○   The *definition* is the customer's needs and expectations (which must be translated into clearly defined and measurable requirements for building projects).

○   The *system* is prevention (which ensures that non-conformance does not occur).

○   The *performance standard* is a 100% achievement of requirements (which means that the only acceptable standard is right first time, every time).

○   The *measure* is the time spent firefighting (which is the cost of not doing things right first time).

If quality is to be achieved in building, all these four fundamental principles must be accepted in both the design and construction processes involved in a building project. Logically, there is no reason why they cannot be accepted, as the essential processes involved are no different to those carried out in other businesses in which these fundamental principles are already in use.

There are, however, a number of factors in current building design and construction practice that may inhibit the acceptance of these principles. In relation to the above four principles these factors can be considered as follows:

○   *Definition.* 'Needs and expectations' must be translated into 'requirements', and it might be argued that it is impossible to define every requirement, particularly those that may have a subjective content (e.g. aesthetic appearance of an external elevation, internal ambience of a particular space enclosure, etc.[30]).

O   *System.* The idea that everything that could go wrong can be prevented from doing so may be difficult to accept as, despite the amount of planning that is carried out, coping with the unplanned and unforeseen is part of the 'culture' of the construction industry.

O   *Performance standard.* The notion of perfection that 100% conformance creates is again extremely difficult to accept because there is a deep-rooted expectation that requirements can never be completely defined and therefore imperfection is inevitable.

O   *Measure.* The fact that mismanagement is almost priced into the total building process (i.e. costings allow for an imperfect output from one phase to the next) means that identifying the cost of *not* doing things right first time is extremely difficult in current design and construction practice[20].

Application of the four fundamentals

The four fundamentals can be applied directly to the process of building design as follows:

O   *Definition.* Any type of requirement for a building's design, or construction requirements to physically achieve that design, is capable of being clearly defined and judged for achievement by either calibration or comparison, and the only reason for failure is that the effort has not been made.

O   *System.* Ensuring that any of the above requirements are met first time, every time through preventing their *not* being met should become a normal part of the planning process throughout the briefing, designing and specifying phases of a building project.

O   *Performance standard.* Meeting requirements 100% is not impossible when it is appreciated that this means meeting them *as and when* they are known, and this concept does not rule out the possibility of the requirements then being changed.

O   *Measure.* The cost of *not* meeting requirements first time can easily be deduced in the building design (and subsequent construction) process by pricing time and resources wasted on any particular project, and possible loss of future commissions.

Any change required to the actual 'philosophical' process of building design can therefore be argued to be not very significant – and indeed many architects and engineers may claim that this is the way that they personally approach their practice. However, if this is the case, but quality problems persist, then some fundamental change must still be required in either the people themselves or the supporting management procedures and methods of process control being applied in the design organizations.

This aspect of applying the fundamentals of quality to building design practice will be dealt with in Chapter 6 and developed in detail in subsequent chapters.

Why a change in attitude is necessary

It can be seen that these fundamentals of quality are more the principles for a philosophy (or way of thinking) rather than for action. In order to embrace these principles the individual designer, and eventually the whole design practice, must really believe them. Paying mere lip-service to these fundamentals and disbelieving them will only engender scepticism about the later process control procedures required in a quality management system.

As it is doubtful that these process control procedures in themselves will increase the motivation of people (especially designers, architects and engineers, who are already self-motivated by the creative nature of their work) there is a danger that the procedures could actually *de*-motivate people, unless they understand and believe the fundamental philosophy.

How and why these four fundamentals should encourage designers to think differently can be suggested as follows:

O   *Definition.* Designing to satisfy clearly defined requirements does not detract from (and may even increase) the challenge of creative design, and passing on clearly defined requirements for construction should go a long way towards ensuring that the design is correctly physically realized.

O   *System.* As planning is so much part of the normal work of a designer, the concept of planning to prevent requirements not being met should not be difficult to embrace.

O   *Performance standard.* Meeting requirements 100% is self-evidently a worthwhile aim.

O   *Measure.* Wasted costs to the practice and the project mean wasted time to the individual designer, which he or she could personally better spend on creative design.

Any change required in the thinking of designers should therefore not detract from their essential concern for creative design, as the application of this philosophy does not impinge upon the creativity of their work. Indeed, it should, if understood correctly, be supportive of their work as designers[31].

Chapter 5

Principles of BS 5750/ISO 9000/EN 29000 quality systems

It is not the intention of this chapter to concentrate too much on the exact 'letter' of the Quality System Standard[5] but rather to abstract its 'spirit' and examine the new rigour that its application to the building design – and subsequent construction – processes will demand. This approach is adopted for three reasons:

○   The construction industry at large – particularly its professional designers – finds the specific language of the Standard itself difficult to interpret and apply to their own current practice.

○   The Standard can only be considered as a minimum requirement for a cost-effective quality management system.

○   The obsession with getting 'certified to a Standard' for outward QA purposes only is peculiar to the UK and is in danger of bringing the quality issue into disrepute. Concentrating too much on the Standard itself might only encourage this approach.

However, the Standard does provide the basic mechanisms of a systematic application which is necessary to support the acceptance of the fundamental philosophy described in Chapter 4.

The requirements of the Standard

The basic requirements of a general quality management system – which can be applied to *any* product or service – are laid down in the British, European and International Standards. The number codes of the parts are different between these standards although the content is exactly the same. The following numbers use the International (ISO) part numbers, as these are the simplest to use for analysing the Standard:

ISO 9001–9003. These sections describe the specification for a quality management system, with 9001 being the most relevant as it is intended for design and production.

ISO 9004. This section describes the guidance for implementing a quality management system for both design and production processes, and does in fact contain much more detailed requirements of a quality management system (e.g. Elements of Design Review) than the specification laid down in 9001.

If a design practice wishes to become certified to the Standard their system will be only assessed against ISO 9001. However, if that practice wants its system to bring about a real cost-effective improvement to its processes, then it is strongly recommended that ISO 9004 should be taken as the guide. Referring to this particular section means that not only would the practice be able to become certified – because it would obviously satisfy the minimum requirements – but it would also be much closer to ensuring that real benefits resulted from its efforts.

The essential requirements of ISO 9004 provide the fundamental mechanisms to support the philosophy of quality described in Chapter 4. In broad terms, the four basic mechanisms of a quality management system as established in ISO 9004 are as follows:

O   *Organization* requires the clear definition of responsibilities and relationships for a total service or product.

O   *Auditing* requires the ability to demonstrate that the tasks defined in the responsibilities are continually being carried out according to stated methods.

O   *Reviewing* requires continuous checks on process methods and action procedures if stated requirements are not being met.

O   *Feedback* requires the tracking of causes of errors that generate defects in measurable terms, so that processes can be improved, non-conformance to requirements reduced and the benefit demonstrated.

These mechanisms can be considered not only as fundamental to the setting up and maintaining of a quality management system itself, but also as the additional formal actions to be carried out in the design process for a building project. That is, a quality management system needs to be constantly reviewed, but formal reviews need to be carried out from time to time throughout the design process of a project.

The detailed applications of each of these mechanisms will be described in subsequent chapters, which relate to the various phases of a building project.

Why the Standard should be applied

The reasons this general Standard for a quality management system should be applied to building design are as follows:

O   The design of buildings as a process is fundamentally no different from that of any other artefact which has technological implications.

O   The Standard views design as an integral part of production and will therefore, by definition, impose on the building design process the appropriate discipline to ensure that what is designed can, in fact, be produced – or, in building terms, constructed.

O   The various processes involved in a building project (briefing, scheme designing, detail designing, specifying, etc.) have very distinct products, and therefore only a very general standard can apply to the building process as a whole.

A comparison of the systematic requirements of the Standard, and the practical control requirements for the building design process, reveals that there is nothing in the latter that is not covered in the former[32]. This point will become clearer as subsequent chapters deal with each phase in detail.

How the interpretation can be made

The practical interpretation of the Standard's requirements to the building design (and subsequent construction) processes needs to take account of the following factors:

O   Although some of the terms and expressions used *seem* only relevant to the design of manufactured products, they are in fact extremely relevant to the design of buildings, which still have to be 'manufactured'. Therefore the importance of meaning should not be lost in changing the words, and the demand for rigour must not be diluted.

O   Relating the process requirements of the Standard to procedural descriptions in building design standard plans of work may help, but these plans of work may not directly support the requirements of a quality management system[33].

There is far more to be gained – and far less to be lost – by making current building design practice more rigorous in order to conform with the Standard's quality management system requirements than by trying to modify (and inevitably dilute) the Standard to suit current *ad hoc* building design practices. This is because many of the clients for which buildings are designed are themselves applying the Standard to their own businesses and are therefore becoming familiar with the terminology. Also, the traditional plans of work currently being (or, in many cases, *not* being) applied do not appear to be able to prevent design-related quality problems occurring in practice, which are only loosely based on formal plans of work. The requirements of a quality management system are intended to control the actual process of design, whereas the plans of work, by definition, only suggest a pattern and sequence of events to be carried during that process. In other words, the plan of work is only *part* of that process – additional elements need to be added to ensure effective control.

The other disadvantage of the plan of work is that it creates the illusion that the building design and construction process can be carried out in straightforwardly *sequential* stages. The reality is that it is a highly *iterative* process, with the need for much interaction between the briefing, designing and specifying phases, and that it is usual for these phases to be continued during construction. The approach of the Standard, and the model described in the next chapter, recognizes the iterative nature of the process, especially the need to consider brief, design and production issues in parallel, and therefore offers a more realistic basis for systematic process control than the traditional plan of work.

Finally, it is paradoxical that the one basic mechanism of a quality management system that is also required in the plan of work (i.e. feedback) is usually omitted in practice for fear of any liability claims that might arise. It is, therefore, interesting that in promoting its own Quality Assessment Scheme[34] the architects' institute is suggesting that feedback on a profession-wide basis should be included in their Scheme in recognition that it is the one mechanism common to both a quality management system and a plan of work that is vital for continuous quality improvement.

Chapter 6

A quality management model for building projects

A model of the total building project process is required because if quality means conformance to requirements then there must be some means of ensuring that an unbroken chain of conformance to requirements exists throughout every phase of the total project process. A fundamental and consistent process analysis model that links the output of any task of any phase forward to subsequent tasks and phases and backward to previous ones provides such a means. This is because the quality of the outcome of any phase – based on how its requirements have been met within that phase – is ultimately dependent on the quality of any other phase for the quality of the total building as a product (e.g. briefing–designing, specifying–constructing, etc.). This will become more clear when each phase is addressed in detail in subsequent chapters.

What the model should represent

A quality management model for building projects was defined during an SERC-funded research project[32] to comprise:
O   The critical phases and tasks needed in the building design and construction process based on the observation of practice.
O   A standard process model that can apply to any design or any other associated process in the project (see Fig. 6.1).
O   The application of the fundamental philosophy and mechanisms of quality as described in previous chapters.
It was felt by the research team that this was the only way of ensuring that the principles of a quality management system could be effectively applied to the building design and construction process.

The model therefore represents a combination of the best quality and project management practice in a way that ensures that the vital element of feedback is taken into account. It also provides a basic and rigorous test against which any corporate or project quality management system could be judged for consistency.

Description of the model

The basic framework of the model outlines six distinct phases in the life of a building project through which a chain of conformance to requirements must be carried out if quality is to be achieved. It is important to note that the term 'phase' does not conform entirely with the word 'stage' used in the RIBA, PSA and BPF Plans of Work[33, 7, 8]. This is because the latter implies a sequence of periods of time which have a beginning and an end, and does not really deal with the problem of interaction over time and between 'stages'.

The term 'phase' therefore means *a particular set of tasks which together will achieve a stated objective* (which could also be considered as a 'function' carried out generally, but not entirely, by *one* project participant), and is distinct in that respect from any other phase. However, although any 'phase' could recur in any subsequent 'phase' (or 'stage' in plan of work terms), the application of the process model requires that every task must logically be carried out, and in the sequence defined by the phase, if the chain of conformance is to remain unbroken. For example, when 'designing' as a phase has to be carried out during 'construction' as a stage, *every* defined task for that phase should still be reconsidered, and so on.

The six identified phases, all of which have distinct objectives, are as follows:

1   Briefing (including procurement)
2   Designing
3   Specifying
4   Tendering
5   Constructing
6   Maintaining (including managing)

An example of the difference between the model 'phase' and a plan of work 'stage' is that briefing can occur during a design, tender, construction or operating stage if there is a change in the client's requirements, or designing can occur in a construction stage if there is a change in the designer's requirements, etc. It will also logically follow from the detailed task analysis in the model that if any particular phase occurs during the life of a project, all subsequent phases must also occur, and the output of any phase could 'feedback' to the input of all or any preceding phases. Finally, logic will demand that maintaining should comprise the continual recurrence of all preceding phases, and briefing cannot occur unless maintaining has been considered in some detail in order to close the ultimate feedback loop.

The phases, their objectives and their basic inputs are shown in Fig. 6.1. This figure is a simplification of series of critical relationships between a number of tasks that lie beneath each phase and repeated inputs to inputs to each of those tasks. In other words, the model can be described as operating down through a series of levels as shown in Fig. 6.2. The highest level of the model (phases) has already been described in Fig. 2.2 and the next level is that of specific tasks in each phase.

Every task has been described so that it can be consistently identified down through each level of the model, either manually or with the use of a computer relational database. A standard package called DATAEASE[35] has been used, but a customized system will eventually be required to cope with the complex and many relationships that need to exist.

The outputs of each task are described in terms familiar to those using plans of work in design and construction practice. Each task contains a description of its essential purpose and is classified as a particular type of task, as this may be relevant to demonstrating the very different input needs and the output of one task compared to another.

An example of a specific task taken from the designing phase is as follows:

No.	B1
Name	USESTUDY
Description	Space use and relationship and appropriate materials
Output	Space use, Material study
Type	Define

Every task has in common the fact that it is distinct from any other task, it is critical to the successful completion of the phase in which it occurs, and its output is an essential part of the input to subsequent tasks – and therefore must be in the correct sequence in its phase.

The tasks identified for each phase and their outputs are as follows.

Briefing 12 tasks A   Feasibility statement
                       A1   Initial brief
                       A10 Adviser appointment
                       A11 Procurement choice
                       A12 Team appointment

Fig 6.1

The quality management model

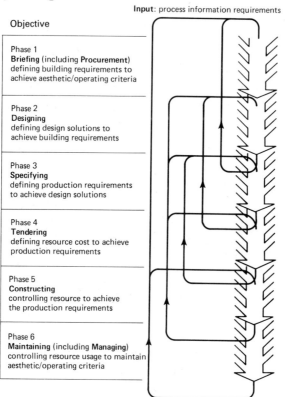

Input: process information requirements

Objective

Phase 1
Briefing (including **Procurement**)
defining building requirements to
achieve aesthetic/operating criteria

Phase 2
Designing
defining design solutions to
achieve building requirements

Phase 3
Specifying
defining production requirements
to achieve design solutions

Phase 4
Tendering
defining resource cost to achieve
production requirements

Phase 5
Constructing
controlling resource to achieve
the production requirements

Phase 6
Maintaining (including **Managing**)
controlling resource usage to maintain
aesthetic/operating criteria

Output: a building that meets the client's aesthetic/operating criteria

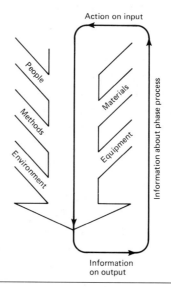

Action on input

Feedback loops
denote the fact that
the 'output' of a phase
may affect the 'input'
of the previous phase
as well as its own
phase

People

Methods

Environment

Materials

Equipment

Information about phase process

Information
on output

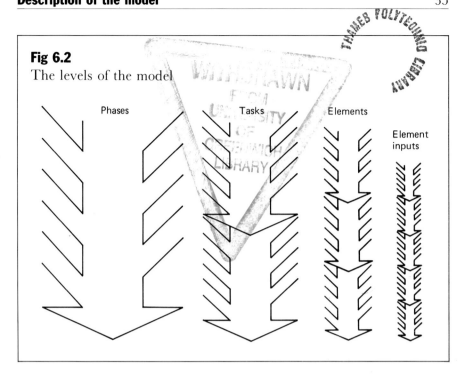

Fig 6.2
The levels of the model

A13 Method statement
A15 Cost/time/grade targets
A16 Context statement
A17 Site study
A18 Building requirements
A19 Method of test for design

This set of tasks comprises the important phase that must precede (but interact with) the designing phase. Briefing must be regarded as a prerequisite and integral function of the design process itself, and must therefore be considered in a quality management system for building design. It is dealt with in detail in Chapter 7.

Designing 12 tasks B   Final brief
                        B1   Space use/material study
                        B10 Alternative solutions
                        B11 Location drawing set
                        B12 Validated scheme design
                        B13 Structure/envelope study
                        B15 Services/fittings study
                        B16 Alternative solutions
                        B17 Detail drawing set

B18   Validated detail design for performance
B19   Final detail design

This set of tasks comprises the essential phase of the design process, and its function is the sole responsibility of the building designer. It is therefore the main activity that a quality management system for building design must address.

As it is generally true that in any project, scheme or 'concept' designing is a prerequisite function of, but integral with, detail designing (the exception being when 'standard' building systems are used[36]), and that as each aspect has a distinct output, they are dealt with separately and in that order in this phase. Therefore, scheme design is dealt with in detail in Chapter 8 and detail design in Chapter 9.

Specifying   12 tasks   C   Constructable design
                             C1   Classification system
                             C10   Information database
                             C11   Contractual requirements
                             C12   Temporary works requirements
                             C13   Accuracy requirements
                             C14   Validated design for construction
                             C15   Procedural specification
                             C16   Technical specification
                             C17   Validated specification
                             C18   Final specification
                             C19   Drawing/specification set

This set of tasks comprises the important phase in which the output of detail designing has to be translated into terms that enable the subsequent tendering and constructing phases to be successfully carried out. As a function, *specifying* must be integral with *detail designing* even though each will have its specific output.

It is important to note the following points about these first three phases:

○   The tasks described in *briefing*, *designing* and *specifying* are those that concern the broadest management level where a quality management system must first be applied. There will be many sub-tasks under each one concerning particular design criteria to be satisfied and material characteristics/specialist trade processes to be taken into account, to which the principles of the model must consistently be applied.

○   These first three phases will be iterative as processes and overlap as 'stages' in practice. This does not mean that, ideally, each task in each phase should not be carried out in the sequence shown above, as this is the only way to ensure that a consistent chain of conformance to requirements is being achieved. For example, if a change occurs in *briefing* during the *specifying phase* – however minor – every subsequent task should be carried out through all three phases. (It is likely that this does not occur in practice for one reason or another, and this omission could be the cause of many quality-related events that are cited in building projects[15].)

○   *Designing* and *specifying* are considered as distinct phases as they have distinct objectives and may require essentially different inputs for their task outputs to be successful. This does not mean that there need not be continual iteration between tasks in both phases (especially detail designing and specifying) for the output of both designing and specifying tasks.

○   Ideally, the first three phases should all be complete before tendering if the objectives of this particular phase are to be achieved.

Tendering   8 tasks   D   Request for proposal
                            D1   Capability report
                            D10   Resource list
                            D11   Specialist list
                            D12   Specialist tenders
                            D13   Priced tender
                            D14   Quality plan

This set of tasks comprises the phase in which the design is effectively costed for production. Although in practice this is not the prime function of the building designer, it does contain elements relevant to the cost estimating of design and design variations and should therefore be considered in a quality management system for building design.

Construction   32 tasks   E   Contract management team
                                E1   Contract management tool
                                E10   Specialist awareness
                                E11   Specialist appointment
                                E12   Accessible site
                                E13   Timely purchase orders
                                E14   Early resource order
                                E15   Key supervisors and operatives
                                E16   Credit facilities
                                E17   Equipment source
                                E18   Serviced site
                                E19   Secure storage

E20 Site layout
E21 Drained site
E22 Roads and services
E23 Supported excavations
E24 Foundations
E25 Ground slab
E26 Superstructure
E27 Floors and staircase
E28 Roof structure
E29 Exterior cladding
E30 Finished roof
E31 Partitioned spaces
E32 First fixings for services
E33 Walls and ceilings
E34 Second fixings for services
E35 Finished floor
E36 Finished decoration
E37 Finished landscape
E38 Finished building
E39 Accepted building

This set of tasks comprises the phase in which the design is physically realized in production. Although it is not the prime function of the building designer, it does contain elements relevant to the 'buildability prediction' of design and design variations, and should therefore be considered in a quality management system for building design. The designing role in the tendering and constructing phases is dealt with in detail in Chapter 11.

Maintaining any or all of the tasks described in preceding phases, depending on the extent of work required.

This phase is the one in which the original design is operated. Although this is not the prime function of the building designer, it does contain elements relevent to the 'decay and decline' of the design and should therefore be considered in a quality management system for building design. In practice, the only real involvement that the design practice can have in this particular phase is if (1) it can take responsibility for the management of the building it has designed or (2) it can become positively involved in the post-occupancy evaluation process of the building it has designed. Then it would be diversifying from the prime function for which it exists and one which is not the prime concern of this book.

The next level of the model is a consistent set of *elements* for each task, which have been described so that they can be related to each task in a computer database or in a manual system. An example of a specific set of elements for a specific task taken from the designing phase is as follows:

No.	B1
Name	USESTUDY
Skills/knowledge	Detail for project/specialists
Performance standard	1st call 68%/2nd 95%/3rd 100%
Procedure	Define unique factors/produce unique statement
Material	Information specific to project/specialists
Facilities/equipment	Information storage/retrieval/application

Every element has in common the fact:
○   It is distinct from any other element.
○   It is critical to the successful completion of the task.
○   Its material input is generally the direct output of the feedforward from a preceding task or the feedback from a subsequent one.

One of the following keywords is always used to define the inputs to each of the distinct elements:

Skills/knowledge	detail
	general
	project
	specialist
Performance standard	correctness
	completeness
	adequacy
Procedure	identify
	define
	select
	compare
	modify
	produce
Material	specific
	general

Facilities/equipment   storage
                            retrieval
                            application
                            representation
                            presentation

Because this model, by definition, is concerned with the management of the building design and construction process (rather than its technology) it is important to note the following points about these elements:

○   Both the *Material* and *Facilities/equipment* element in every task in every phase must be concerned with *information* and *information technology*, manual or computer methods.

○   The term 'specialist' will refer to any project participant who makes a specific contribution, such as client, consultant, sub-contractor, component manufacturer, regulator, etc.

○   The term 'project' refers to the particular building to be developed.

○   The terms used with *Procedure* have very particular meanings (for instance, 'select' means 'to choose from a known range', whereas 'compare' means 'to equate against a common framework', etc.).

○   The most difficult concept is *Performance standard*, which, to comply with the Crosby/Mortiboys fundamental 'system' of 'quality', must always be 100% correct, complete or adequate. However, this is the way in which every *Performance standard* element must be considered if the model is to be true to its origins.

In building design and construction practice, a deficiency in any of the inputs of any particular element would be a reduced level of whatever is described as the ideal situation and would result in a 'defect' in the output of the particular task. ('Defect' is the popular term given to a fault identified in either the design or construction practice of the industry[18] and for which designers and contractors may be liable.)

A defect in the output of a task will then have the effect of causing a deficiency in the input of an element in another task, either in the same or subsequent phase. If that particular task also has deficiencies in the inputs to its other elements then the effect may be compounded, the individual deficiencies difficult to trace and the total cause impossible to remedy.

The final level of the model has been devised to overcome this 'tracing' problem and takes each specific element and further decomposes it to a similar set of element details. Therefore under each element, the same element details are repeated in the order as follows:

The 'skills/knowledge' of *Skills/knowledge* is   *tutoring*
The 'performance standard' of *Performance standard* is   *measurement*
The 'procedure' of *Procedure* is   *formality*
The 'material' of *Material* is   *software*
The 'facilities/equiment' of *Facilities/equipment* is   *hardware*

Taking the specific task used previously as an example, the element details are as follows:

No.   B1
Name   USESTUDY
Skills/knowledge

Tutoring	Instruction in topics related to project specialists
Examination	Test of understanding
Study course	Training for individual
Software	Training material
Hardware	Training material access means

Performance standard

Metrology	An objective method of calibrating calls for information
Measurement	A calibrated value
Measuring	An application of the value
Software	Calibration material
Hardware	Calibration material access means

Procedure

Systems analysis	An objective method of describing building use
Analysis	A use description method
Formality	A description structure
Software	Description material
Hardware	Description material access means

Material

Information science	An objective method of structuring/processing information
Current	An up-to-date use
Processing	An information method use
Software	Method material
Hardware	Method material access means

Facilities/equipment

Purchasing	An objective method of obtaining equipment

Specification   A performance use
Using/caring   A use/care experience
Software   Experience material
Hardware   Experience material access means

Each element now has its own specific set of element details, which are in effect the inputs to each input in each task. A deficiency in any one or more of these element details will be the cause of the deficiency in the element, which in turn will have caused the defect in the output of the task.

It can now be seen from the descriptions that whereas each *element* input to a task was a project-related function, each *element detail* is a corporate-related function, i.e. a lack of a specific skill or knowledge by a particular project participant is the fault of the corporate organization involved, not the person.

This means that the cause of any deficiency can be traced down through the various levels of the model to the client organization, design practice or construction company to which the particular participant(s) responsible for a defective task belong. This is particularly useful in devising and testing a quality management system for a building project, because the system must ultimately work for the separate organizations taking part in that project.

Application of the model in design practice

The model was devised by an experienced research team, with a practical working knowledge of building design and construction practice, who studied the principles and application of quality management to the industry over a three-year period. They recognize that the model is complex (at its final level it is broken down into some 1900 separate element detail inputs over the briefing to constructing phases), but nevertheless believe that it will only be through such a fundamental approach that quality management can be effectively applied to the design (and subsequent construction) phases of a building project. However, in the short term there may be great difficulty in trying to apply these fundamental concepts, and the consequential changes, to such a traditional industry.

Therefore the following chapters will take the essential features from various levels of the model and relate them to the familiar functions of design practice through the various phases of a building project. In this way, it is hoped that the integrity of the model can be maintained and its immediate (if only limited) application to practice can begin to realize the consequential cost-effective raising of standards.

Guide to reading Chapters 7–11

Any quality management system for a design practice, construction company and client organization, and any quality plan for a project, can use this model as a basis for identifying the cause of errors in any task to bring about continuous quality improvement in meeting the client's requirements. The most detailed level of the model finally traces the cause of any deficiency (in an element input to a task) to a deficiency in the element detail input to the element itself. In this way the cause of a corporate management deficiency can be identified and corrected so that no defect in the project management output of a task will occur.

In Fig. 6.3 the question should be asked: 'Which element input will be deficient if the output of the task is defective?' Eventually the answer will be, say, 'Skills/knowledge' (or 'Procedure' or 'Performance standard' or 'Information' or 'Information technology' or a combination or any two or more), so then we trace the cause in the detail input to each element.

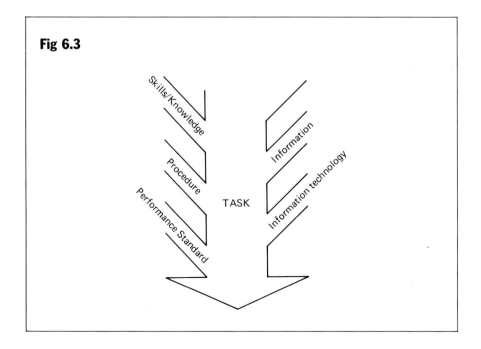

Fig 6.3

Each element has its own set of detail inputs, which in effect is a repeat of the same set of element inputs but now applied in a more detailed way at a deeper level of process definition. In Fig. 6.4 the question should be asked: 'Which detail will be deficient if the element input itself is deficient?' Any deficiency in any of the above detail inputs

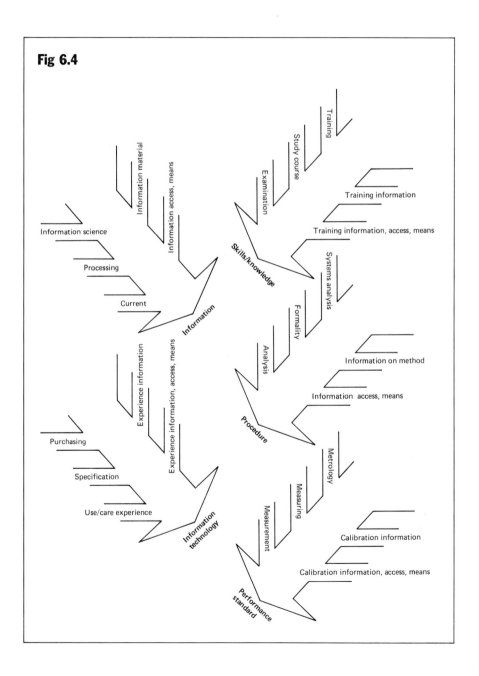

Fig 6.4

can only be corrected by a change in the *corporate management* practice of the design practice, construction company or client organization responsible for the particular element input identified.

Chapter 7

The briefing phase

Briefing has long been recognized as the critical activity that begins the building project process. It is emphasized in the RIBA Plan of Work, in which the architect as building designer must elicit the brief from the client before any design activity can begin[35].

Current research into briefing is addressing the problem from a construction project management point of view and seeing if there are better ways of getting the potential client to understand his building needs and to communicate those needs to the building project design and management team[37]. A recently published guide on briefing by the BRE outlines a systematic approach to the activity, and many of the following 'critical' tasks from the model were based on its sugge- stions[38]. A joint academic/industry study on the 'construction management/management contracting' forms of building procurement is also addressing the problem with the intention of producing guidance on the technical and procedural aspects of the subject[39]. Also, of course, because of the increasing complexity of modern building design and management methods, specialist consultancies now exist to provide a client briefing service[40].

How, then, does the model view this particular phase of the process? What are the critical tasks and their outputs? How can the key inputs be free of deficiencies? Who, of all the project participants, is responsible?

What are the critical tasks?

As with each phase of the model, a number of critical tasks have been identified. It is proposed that these tasks may still only be the 'heads' of a set of sub-tasks beneath them, the number of which will vary from project to project, and from task to task (e.g. the task 'A18 Building requirements' will have many sub-tasks and even sub-sub-tasks beneath its 'head'). The point is that only if these critical 'head' tasks begin with the appropriate inputs is it possible for the sub-tasks beneath them to have appropriate inputs in their turn.

The specific critical 'head' tasks (the name of which describes their essential output) that must be carried out in order to ensure that technical and procedural briefing requirements are clearly defined, communicated and measurable for achievement are as follows:

A   Feasibility statement
A1   Initial brief
A10   Adviser appointment
A11   Procurement choice
A12   Team appointment
A13   Roles statement
A14   Method statement
A15   Cost/time/grade targets
A16   Context statement
A17   Site study
A18   Building requirements
A19   Method of test for design

Before the nature of these tasks and their inputs through the various levels of the model are examined, it will be useful to see what the Quality Systems Standard[5] suggests as the elements of this particular phase. In ISO 9004 the part that most mirrors the briefing phase in building design is under the heading of 'Quality in Marketing', which essentially requires the supplier to:

O   Determine the need for . . .

O   Define demand and sector for . . . in order to determine the grade, quantity, price and timing estimates.

O   Determine customer requirements by review . . . assess any unstated expectations or biases held by customer.

O   Communicate customer requirements clearly within company.

O   Provide a product brief that translates customer requirements and expectations into a preliminary set of specifications for design work that include:
— Environmental, usage, and reliability performance character-istics.
— Style, colour, sensory characteristics.
— Installation, configuration or fit.
— Applicable standards and regulations.

— Packaging.

— Quality assurance/verification.

o   Establish an information monitoring and feedback system on a continuous basis . . . determine extent and nature of problems in relation to customer experience and expectations . . . provide clues to possible design change . . . management action.

Although these principles refer to the supply of a product or service to a customer in the marketplace, it is easy to see how they can also relate to a building and a client. The only point that does not seem appropriate is packaging, although in terms of building design this could refer to the way that proposed design solutions are presented to the client. The concept that 'style' should be clearly identified as a client requirement, rather than being left solely to the designer to create as part of the solution, might seem foreign to traditional building design practice, although style requirements are often implicitly stated by the local planning authorities and even by the client body itself.

The establishment of a formal feedback system for the project tends not to be part of current building design practice for reasons stated in Chapter 5. However, unless this *is* set up in the future it will be difficult for any design practice to claim that it is implementing a quality management system.

Bearing in mind the above elements of a quality management system (which *must* be used if formal QA is to be obtained for the design practice) and the stated objective of the model's briefing phase shown in Fig. 7.2, the element inputs to each of the tasks that comprise this particular phase can be considered in terms of the criticality of deficiencies in inputs and the likely consequences.

In Fig. 7.1 it can be seen that feedback loops into this phase come from various task outputs in the maintaining and designing phases. The elements on the right-hand side are concerned with those inputs that affect how the information of requirements is both formulated and handled. This is the information that will begin to accumulate from the client's initial idea to build, and will finally develop into a fully documented brief against which any building design proposal can be compared for satisfaction (i.e. going from task A, *Feasibility statement*, to A19, *Method of test for design*).

For example, a deficiency in the project-specific information in task A will result in a defect in the output of the feasibility statement, and this statement in turn will become a deficient part of a number of the information inputs to subsequent tasks, which in their turn will have a defective output.

On the other hand, a deficiency in the general information about the particular type of building the client has in mind (e.g. legislation about

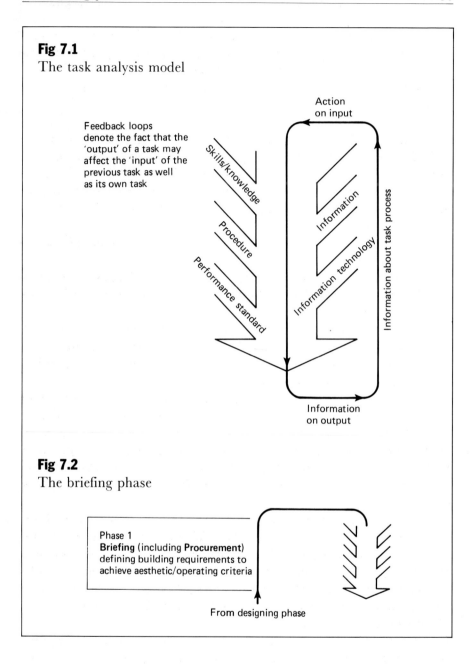

Fig 7.1
The task analysis model

Fig 7.2
The briefing phase

office accommodation) would also result in a defective feasibility statement, which would then become a deficient information input to subsequent tasks because the implications of meeting these particular legislation requirements had not been taken into account.

Even though the information itself may not be deficient, the means of information handling, in terms of storage, retrieval, application and presentation, may well be. This problem, and the way the computer may be used to solve it, has been recognized for many years in academic studies[46, 47].

Essentially, the problem of information handling in a building project stems from the fact that a great number of different participants – all with diverse interests in the project and diverse ways of thinking – are involved over a comparatively long period of time. This results in the need to appropriately utilize different media between participants at different times throughout the project as the information itself changes in type and detail.

The problem of information handling is the most acute in the briefing phase of a building project because:

O   The client usually comprises a diversity of financial and functional interests even before any of the construction industry participants become involved.

O   No drawn or scale model of a building design yet exists to give all participants some basis upon which to communicate information.

O   The means of information handling to suit all likely future project participants may itself still be evolving.

However, deficiencies in this particular element input will also result in a defective output to any of the briefing phase tasks. For instance, in task A15, *Cost/time/grade targets*, if grade targets for aesthetic appearance and functional performance requirements of any part of the proposed building cannot be adequately presented as an output, then the information input of the subsequent task A18, *Building requirements*, will be deficient.

In Fig. 7.1 the elements on the left-hand side are concerned with the people inputs in terms of their 'skills and knowledge', 'procedures' (i.e. the way in which a particular participant works) and 'performance standard' (i.e. the appropriate level of attainment that is expected of a particular individual carrying out the task). Deficiencies in any of these element inputs can therefore have a great variety of generic causes, some of which could be as follows:

O   A lack of either skill or knowledge (or both) by individual(s) for a particular task, as a result of appointing the wrong person to carry it out.

O   A lack of an appropriate procedure as a result of following traditional professional or commercial practices which are inappropriate to the task required for a particular project.

O   A lack of conviction in the ability to reach a particular performance standard for a specific task, due to an inherent cultural attitude of a sector of the construction industry.

In the briefing phase, for instance, a deficiency in the knowledge input in task A10, *Adviser appointment*, will result in a defective output, which in turn will cause a deficient information input to task A12, *Team appointment*, the defective output of which will cause skill and knowledge deficiencies in many subsequent tasks in briefing as well as all subsequent phases. Another example is that a deficiency in either procedure or performance standard inputs into task A19, *Method of test for design*, would result in a weak test as the output, which in turn becomes deficient information into many of the tasks in the subsequent designing and specification phases.

Bearing these likely causes of deficiencies in mind, the ideal element inputs to every task in the briefing phase is shown in Schedule 1 below, and the relationship of each task to the others is in Fig. 7.3.

Why controlled feedback is important

Controlled feedback loops are needed not only within the briefing phase itself to maintain consistency in meeting requirements but also from the maintaining (including managing) phase. The feedback will need to supply the following information:

1   The briefing implications for building maintenance (including management) in terms of:

(a)   The operational requirements as a managed facility for a particular use or uses.

(b)   The operational requirements as a managed facility for particular changes in the use or uses.

(c)   The cost/time/grade requirements as a maintained facility for a particular use or uses.

(d)   The cost/time/grade requirements as a maintained facility for particular changes in the use or uses.

This information will have to be derived from the 'detail project' skills/knowledge and 'general for specialists' information inputs to be used in the maintaining (including managing) phase by the client or his or her representative.

2   The actual managing and maintaining consequence on the building operation of the finally constructed design evolved from the briefing phase. This information will have to be derived from the 'detail project' skills/knowledge and 'specific' information used in the maintaining (including managing) phase by the client or end user.

Unless the feedback can exist for (1) above, the information and/or skills/knowledge inputs to any head task or sub-task that contains elements of *targets* (A15), *context* (A16), *site*(A17), *requirements* (A18) and

Fig 7.3

The briefing tasks and feedback loops (showing the critical feedback loops from subsequent to preceding tasks *within* the phase)

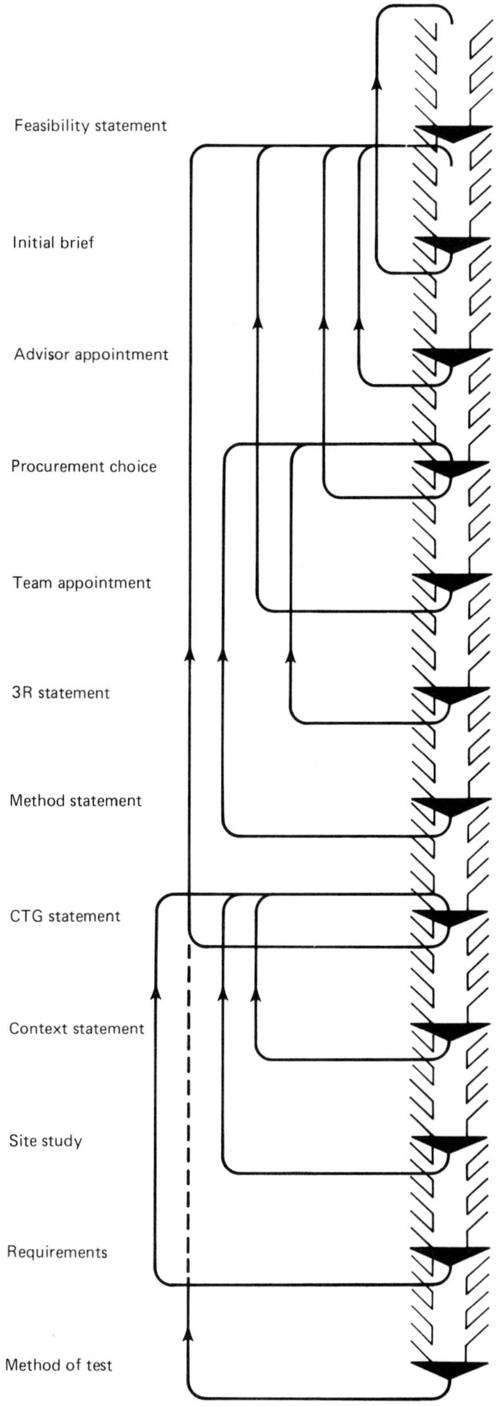

Feasibility statement

Initial brief

Advisor appointment

Procurement choice

Team appointment

3R statement

Method statement

CTG statement

Context statement

Site study

Requirements

Method of test

test (A19) will be deficient. It must also be accepted that the feedback for
(2), which is ideally necessary to support the feedback for (1), can only
come through the rigorous monitoring of similar buildings in use.
Because of the uniqueness of building projects and the client passing the
buildings onto end users outside their control, this is seldom undertaken
at present.

Who carries out the tasks?

The project participants responsible for making inputs to each of the
head tasks (and therefore any sub-task under that heading) are as
follows:

A   *Feasibility statement* – the client.
A1   *Initial brief* – the client.
A10   *Adviser appointment* – the client.
A11   *Procurement choice* – the client and the manager.
A12   *Team appointment* – the client and the manager.
A13   *Roles statement* – the client, the manager, the architect/interior/
      structural/services designers and specialist contractors (if ap-
      pointed).
A14   *Method statement* – as A13.
A15   *Cost/time/grade targets* – as A13.
A16   *Context statement* – the manager and architect/designer.
A17   *Site study* – the architect/structural/services designers.
A18   *Building requirements* – as A13.
A19   *Method of test for design* – as A13.

Unless these participants make a responsible contribution to the above
tasks as allocated, the skills/knowledge inputs will all be deficient.

Overcoming current problem areas in this phase

The particular problems in current practice that have to be overcome to
eliminate input deficiencies in the tasks of the briefing phase are as
follows:
1   The briefing phase is concerned with those aspects of a building
project where both technical and procedural requirements are primarily
determined. The determination is made initially by the client, but very
soon in the project these requirements are influenced by the client's
prime advisers, and today the architect/designer is not necessarily one of

these. In the ideal task sequence shown above, *all* the designers – and the specialist contractors who make a design contribution – should both be appointed *and* make a contribution to determining the requirements for the cost/time/grade targets. Also, when the requirements for the building are later being determined in the light of the context statement and site study, and fed back, these original target requirements may have to be amended.

2   Even if these particular aspects are determined and appropriately amended at the right time and in the right sequence, the fact that each project demands its own unique combination of procedural and technical requirements means that their *exact* determination may be difficult. Also, the people who will be most concerned about the determination of the technical requirements for the building and its operation (i.e. the end users) are not usually involved in the briefing phase of a building project unless the client or architect makes a special effort to ensure that they are, but even this is only possible if the end users can be easily identified.

The suggested answers to these problems are the following changes to current building design practice:

O   *All* requirements and their acceptance criteria should be rigorously determined *and* agreed between the client (and preferably the end user) and the designers, manager and, where appropriate, any specialist contractors as an essential part of the briefing phase.

O   The client must take responsibility for defining the end-user requirements, as he is the participant responsible for initiating the building project and making the judgements about the building as a product and how it should satisfy the needs of the customer in the marketplace.

O   The architect/designer primarily, and then the other designers subsequently, must take responsibility for the interpretation of the client/end user requirements into technical requirements in the briefing phase, prior to the designing phase commencing.

Unless these changes are implemented in curent building client procurement and design practice it is likely that the skills/knowledge and information inputs to the head tasks (and all sub-tasks) will continue to be deficient, with resulting defects in the outputs. It follows that the information inputs to the tasks in the subsequent designing (scheme and detail) and specifying phases will be deficient.

Schedule 1 below indicates each element input to each task of the briefing phase and, when read in conjunction with Figs 6.3 and 6.4, will further indicate the element detail input to each element. The purpose of Schedule 1 is to guide the reader in planning to prevent deficiencies occurring in the briefing phase of the project. Deficiencies will be prevented if:

1   Every task is always carried out, and always carried out in the logically defined sequence.
2   The description is always borne in mind when the task is being carried out, as this is its essential purpose.
3   The element inputs are always appropriate to the specific task in question in terms of a project management application.
4   The element detail inputs are always appropriate to and in place for the specific element in question in terms of corporate management support.
5   The output is not expected to be anything more or anything less than is stated.

If defects have occurred in this particular phase in past projects, the cause can be traced through the task to the element and finally to the element detail.

Schedule 1: Briefing

No.	A	
Description	Identify aims, resources and context of project	
Inputs	*Skills/knowledge*	General for project/specialist
	Performance standard	Correct interpretation 100%
	Procedure	Analyse initial statement/ evaluate/produce report
	Materials	Information on similar projects/ specialists
	Facilities/equipment	Information storage/retrieval/ application
Output	FEASIBILITY STATEMENT	

No.	A1	
Description	An initial brief emphasizing aims and problems	
Inputs	*Skills/knowledge*	Detail for project/general for specialists
	Performance standard	1st call 68%/2nd call 95%/3rd call 100%
	Procedure	Define unique factors/produce unique statement
	Materials	Information specific to project/ general for specialists
	Facilities/equipment	Information storage/retrieval/ application

Output   INITIAL BRIEF

No.   A10
Description Appointing prime advisers
Inputs   *Skills/knowledge*   Detail for project/specialists
                 Performance standard   Completeness/correctness 100%
                 Procedure   Select specialists/conditions of
                                           engagement
                 Materials   Information specific to specialists
                 Facilities/equipment   Information
                                           storage/retrieval/application
Output   ADVISER APPOINTMENT

No.   A11
Description Procurement method selection
Inputs   *Skills/knowledge*   Detail for project/general for
                                           specialists
                 Performance standard   Correctness 100%
                 Procedure   Select method/modify for project
                 Materials   Information specific to project/
                                           general for methods
                 Facilities/equipment   Information storage/retrieval/
                                           application
Output   PROCUREMENT CHOICE

No.   A12
Description A project team
Inputs   *Skills/knowledge*   Detail for project/general for
                                           specialist
                 Performance standard   Correctness 100%
                 Procedure   Select specialists' contractual
                                           arrangements
                 Materials   Information specific to project/
                                           specialist
                 Facilities/equipment   Information application/
                                           representation
Output   TEAM APPOINTMENT

No.   A13
Description Roles, responsibilities and relationships of team and
                 client

Inputs	*Skills/knowledge*	Detail for project/specialists
	Performance standard	Adequacy – 100%
	Procedure	Define unique factors/produce unique statment
	Materials	Information specific to project/specialists
	Facilities/equipment	Information application/representation
Output	3R STATEMENT	

No.	A14	
Description	Method of working and means of communication	
Inputs	*Skills/knowledge*	Detail for project/specialist
	Performance standard	Adequacy – 100%
	Procedure	Define unique factors/produce unique statement
	Materials	Information specific to project/specialists
	Facilities/equipment	Information application/representation
Output	METHOD STATEMENT	

No.	A15	
Description	Cost, time and grade targets and priorities	
Inputs	*Skills/knowledge*	Detail for project/general for specialists
	Performance standard	Adequacy – 100%
	Procedure	Define unique factors/produce unique statement
	Materials	Information specific to project/general for specialists
	Facilities/equipment	Information retrieval/application/representation
Output	CTG STATEMENT	

No.	A16	
Description	Legal, political and environmental constraints	
Inputs	*Skills/knowledge*	Detail for project/general for specialists
	Performance standard	Correctness – 100%

	Procedure	Define unique factors/produce unique statement
	Materials	Information specific to project/ general for specialists
	Facilities/equipment	Information retrieval/application/ representation
Output	CONTEXT STATEMENT	

No.	A17	
Description	Physical constraints of building site	
Inputs	*Skills/knowledge*	Detail for project/general for specialists
	Performance standard	Correctness – 100%
	Procedure	Define unique factors/produce unique statement
	Materials	Information specific to project/ manual for specialists
	Facilities/equipment	Information retrieval/application/ representation
Output	SITE STUDY	

No.	A18	
Description	Space, fabric, services and fittings requirements	
Inputs	*Skills/knowledge*	Detail for project/specialists
	Performance standard	1st call 68%/2nd call 95%/3rd call 100%
	Procedure	Define unique factors/produce unique statement
	Materials	Information specific to project/ specialists
	Facilities/equipment	Information retrieval/application/ representation
Output	REQUIREMENTS	

No.	A19	
Description	Method of assessment of design meeting requirements	
Inputs	*Skills/knowledge*	Detail for project/specialist
	Performance standard	Adequacy – 100%
	Procedure	Analyse unique factors/produce test method
	Materials	Information specific to project/ specialists
	Facilities/equipment	Information application/ representation/presentation
Output	METHOD OF TEST	

Chapter 8

The designing phase – scheme

Some basic theoretical models of how designers carry out the actual process of designing were described in Chapter 1. It is not the intention to suggest any more theories, or even to question too deeply those that already exist. It is sufficient that all of them – and their modification by observation of practice[23, 24] – show enough similarities to define an essential process to which the principles of quality management can be applied.

Whether the process of designing buildings theoretically comprises the functions of analysis–synthesis–evaluation, analysis–synthesis–verification, conjecture–refutation, etc., the essential process is one in which proposals in terms of design solutions are being made and assessed against requirements for a building.

The reason for considering 'scheme' and then 'detail' designing in separate chapters (although they are considered as *one* phase in terms of the model) is that it is the order in which they occur in practice, and the requirements to be met in each are essentially different. The only exception to this order that might be considered is where a 'standard' constructional system[36] is to be used, and it could be argued that much of the detail designing has been completed before the scheme designing begins. However, even in this situation, both the scheme and detail design of the building have essentially different requirements to satisfy.

Scheme designing is concerned with the creation of a building 'form', which comprises its shape, size and arrangement of spaces and elements, and its internal and external 'material finish' to its elemental parts[19]. Scheme designs have to take into account the following factors:

○   The appearance of the existing natural and built environments.
○   The topology of the site in terms of slope and natural features.

O   The location of the site in terms of access and orientation.
O   The size and location of the site in terms of the ratio of building to external works.
O   The space configuration in terms of activities, relationships and circulation.
O   The space configuration and element composition in terms of thermal, ventilation, day- and sunlight, acoustics, fire, health, safety and security performance.
O   The space configuration and element composition in terms of architectural style.

Scheme design proposals are traditionally presented through scale drawings, models and supporting 'non-graphical' data[43] for assessing requirement satisfaction and – if agreed – developing into detail design and specification for construction.

How, then, does the model view this particular phase of the process? What are the critical tasks and their outputs? How can the key inputs be free of deficiencies? Who, of all the project participants, is responsible?

What are the critical tasks?

As with each phase of the model, a number of critical tasks have been identified. It is proposed that these tasks are only the heads of a set of sub-tasks beneath them, the number of which will vary from project to project and from task to task (e.g. task B1, *Space use/material study*, will have many sub- and even sub-sub-tasks beneath its head). The point is that only if these critical head tasks begin with the appropriate inputs is it possible for the sub-tasks beneath them to have appropriate inputs. This, however, can only occur if the consistency and integrity of the model approach is itself carried through.

The specific critical head tasks (the name of which is their essential output) that must be carried out to ensure that the defined scheme design solution(s) can be demonstrated to meet the defined building requirements derived from the briefing phases are as follows:

B   Final brief
B1   Space use/material study
B10   Alternative solutions
B11   Location drawing set
B12   Validated scheme design
B13   Final scheme design

Before the nature of these tasks and their inputs through the levels of the model are examined it is necessary to see what the Quality System Standard[5] suggests as principles for this particular phase. In ISO 9004, the part that most mirrors the scheme designing phase as well as the detail designing and specifying phases in *building* design is under the heading of 'Quality in Specification and Design', which essentially requires the supplier to:

O   Translate the customer's needs from the product (i.e. the building) brief into technical specifications for materials, products and processes.

O   Provide customer satisfaction at an acceptable price.

O   Provide a product (i.e. the building) that is producible, verifiable and controllable under the proposed production, installation, commissioning or operational conditions.

O   Assign responsibilities for various design duties to activities inside and/or outside the organization.

O   Ensure that design functions provide clear and definitive technical data for procurement, the execution of work and verification of conformance.

O   Establish time-phased design programmes with checkpoints (design reviews or evaluations) appropriate to the product's (i.e. the building's) application, design complexity, extent of innovation and technology being introduced, degree of standardization and similarity with proven designs.

O   Give due consideration to requirements relating to safety, environment and other regulations, including items . . . which may go beyond existing statutory requirements.

O   Ensure that aspects of the design are unambiguous and adequately define important characteristics . . . acceptance and rejection criteria . . . fitness for purpose and safeguard against misuse . . . reliability, maintainability and serviceability through a reasonable life expectancy, including benign failure and safe disposability, as appropriate.

O   Specify methods of measurement and test during both design and production (i.e. construction) phases, including:

—   Performance target values, tolerances and attribute features.

—   Acceptance and rejection criteria.

—   Test and measurement methods, equipment, bias and precision requirements, and computer software considerations.

O   Provide periodic evaluation . . . by fault tree analysis, risk assessment, inspection or test prototypes models and/or production (i.e. construction) samples, amount and degree of testing related to risks identified. Independent testing may be employed to verify tests . . . adequate number of samples to provide statistical confidence . . . Tests to include following activities:

— Evaluation of performance, durability, safety, reliability and maintainability under expected . . . operational conditions.
— Verify that all design features are as intended and that all authorized design changes have been accomplished and recorded.
— Validation of computer systems and software.

O Results of all tests and evaluations are documented regularly throughout the qualification test cycle . . . review of test results should include defect and failure analysis.

O Carry out formal, documented, systematic and critical design reviews at each phase of the design development . . . distinguished from progress meetings primarily concerned with time and cost . . . Participants should represent all functions appropriate to phase being reviewed . . . should identify and anticipate problem areas and inadequacies, and initiate corrective actions to ensure that the final design and supporting data meet customer requirements . . . As appropriate to phase and product (i.e. the building), design reviews should include:

— Items pertaining to customer needs and satisfaction.
— Items pertaining to product (i.e. the building) specification and service requirements.
— Items pertaining to process (i.e. construction) specification and service requirements. (An example of a design review and all its appropriate elements is shown in Chapter 19.)

O Undertake design verification, if necessary, independently or in support of design reviews by:

— Alternative calculations, made to verify the original calculations and analyses.
— Testing by model or prototype.
— Independent verification, to verify the correctness of the original calculations and/or other design activities.

O Appropriately document the results of the final design review in specifications and drawings that define the design baseline, where appropriate including description of qualification test units 'as built' and modified to correct deficiencies. Approve at appropriate levels of management to signify concurrence that design can be realized.

O Provide for a review to determine whether production (i.e. construction) capability and field support (i.e. operation of building) are adequate for new or redesigned product (i.e. building).

O Provide a procedure for controlling the release, change and use of documents that define the design baseline and for authorizing the necessary work to be performed to implement changes that may affect the product (i.e. building) during its entire life cycle. Provide for various necessary approvals, specific points and times for implementing changes, removing obsolete drawings, verification that changes are made at apointed times and places, handling emergency changes necessary to prevent production (i.e. construction) of non-conforming product (i.e. building) . . . Consideration given to formal design reviews and validation testing when the magnitude, complexity or risk associated with the change warrant such actions.

O   Perform periodic re-evaluation of product (i.e. building) in order to ensure that the design is still valid with respect to all specified requirements, including a review of customer needs and technical specification in the light of field (i.e. building in operation) experience, performance surveys or new technology or techniques . . . The need for design change is fed back for analysis . . . care taken that design changes do not cause product (i.e. building) degradation and that proposed changes are evaluated for their impact on all product characteristics in the design baseline definition.

As with briefing, these principles can equally refer to the *client* and the *building* as they do to the '*customer*' and '*product*' when the process of designing is being considered. Where the reader might have some difficulty in relating *product* in the Standard to *building* in design practice, these particular relationships have been suggested by the author. Those aspects of the demands of the Standard – which has initially been written with the manufacturing industries in mind – that appear to be at variance with current building design practice seem to be as follows:

O   The demand for extensive design review, verification and change control procedures – because the manufacturing industry is concerned with producing many repeat products from the same design – may seem excessive and uneconomical for the situation in building design, where only one product is produced from the design.

O   The implicit ability of the design organization to have some direct control or influence over the production of the product, as this is what parts of the reviews will be considering, is *not* the usual situation in current procurement methods.

O   The last demand for *re*-qualification of the design once the product is in the field (which equates to the architect re-assessing the design when the building is in operation) is difficult because:

—   The formal feedback required at the end of a building project is not part of current design practice for the reasons stated in Chapter 5.

—   The fact the designed product in the case of a building is a one-off makes the value of re-qualification seem questionable.

Bearing in mind the above elements of a quality management system (which *must* be used if formal QA is to be obtained for the design practice) and the stated objective of the model's designing phase shown

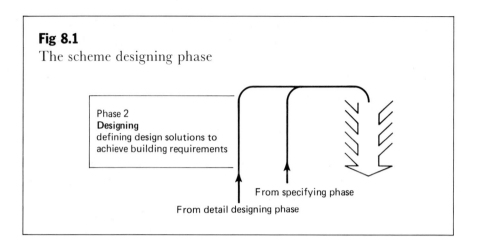

Fig 8.1
The scheme designing phase

Phase 2
Designing
defining design solutions to
achieve building requirements

From specifying phase
From detail designing phase

in Fig. 8.1, the element inputs to each of the tasks that comprise this particular phase can be considered in terms of the criticality of deficiencies in inputs and the likely consequences. In Fig. 8.1 it can be seen that feedback loops into this phase come from various task outputs in the specifying and constructing phases and task outputs from this phase feedback into the briefing phase. The elements on the right-hand side are concerned with those inputs that affect how the information of requirements is both formulated and handled. This is the information that will begin to accumulate from the designer's initial idea of a solution to the brief, and will finally develop into a fully documented scheme design that can be compared for satisfaction against the developed brief, i.e. going from task B, *Final brief*, to B13, *Final scheme design*.

For example, a deficiency in the project-specific information in task B will result in a defect in the output of the final brief, and this brief in turn will become a deficient part of a number of the information inputs to subsequent tasks, which in their turn will have a defective output.

On the other hand, a deficiency in the general information about the particular type of building the client has in mind (e.g. legislation about office accommodation) would also result in a defective final brief, which would then become a deficient information input to subsequent tasks because the implications of meeting these particular legislation requirements had not been taken into account.

Even though the information itself may not be deficient, the means of information technology (in terms of storage, retrieval, application, presentation and presentation) may well be. Essentially, the problem of information technology in the building design process stems from the fact that a number of different designers and advisers – all with diverse interests in the project and ways of thinking – are involved over a comparatively long period of time as the scheme design develops (i.e. architect, interior designer, structural and services designers, legislators, etc.). This results in the need to be able to appropriately utilize different media between the designers, advisers and client(s) at different times throughout the scheme design process as the information itself changes in type and detail.

The problem of information technology should become less acute in the designing than in the briefing phase of a building project because:

O   The client has started to resolve the diversity of interests he has in order to provide a single representation to the construction industry participants as they become involved.

O   Some drawn design (and perhaps scale models) exists which gives all the designers, advisers and client(s) some basis upon which to communicate information.

O   The means of information technology to suit all likely future project participants will have started to evolve.

However, deficiencies in this particular element input will also result in a defective output to any of the designing phase tasks. For instance, in task B10, *Alternative solutions*, if the *alternative implications* in terms of satisfying aesthetic appearance and functional performance requirements of the external envelope of the proposed building cannot be adequately presented as an output, then the information input of the subsequent task B11, *Location drawing set*, will be deficient. This means that, in turn, the information input to task B12, *Validated scheme design*, will be deficient, etc.

In Fig. 8.1 the elements on the left-hand side are concerned with the 'people' inputs in terms of their skills and knowledge, procedures (i.e. the way in which a particular designer works) and performance standard (i.e. the appropriate level of attainment that is expected of a particular individual carrying out the task). Deficiencies in any one of these element inputs can therefore have a great variety of generic causes, some of which could be as follows:

O   A lack of either skill or knowledge (or both) by individual(s) for a particular task as a result of appointing the wrong person to carry it out.

O   A lack of an appropriate procedure as a result of following traditional professional or commercial practices which are inappropriate to the task required for a particular project.

O   A lack of conviction in the ability to reach a particular performance standard for a specific task, due to an inherent cultural attitude of a sector of the construction industry.

In the designing phase, for instance, a deficiency in the knowledge input in task B1, *Space use/material study*, will result in a defective output, which in turn will cause a deficient information input to task B10,

Alternative solutions the defective output of which will cause information deficiencies in all the subsequent tasks in the designing phase. Another example is that a deficiency in either procedure or performance standard inputs into task B13, *Final scheme design*, would result in an uncertain output, which in turn becomes deficient information into many of the tasks in the subsequent detail designing and specification phases.

Fig 8.2

The scheme designing tasks (showing the critical feedback loops from subsequent to preceding tasks *within* the phase)

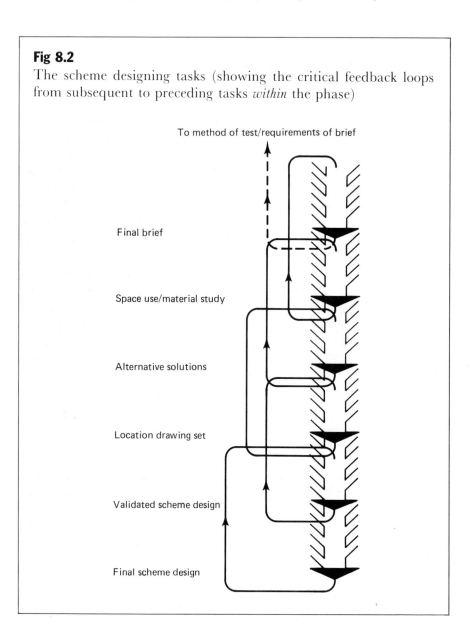

Bearing these likely causes of deficiencies in mind, the ideal element inputs to every task in the designing phase is shown in Schedule 2 below, and the relationship of each task to the other is outlined in Fig. 8.2.

Why controlled feedback is important

Controlled feedback loops are needed not only within the scheme designing phase itself to maintain consistency in meeting requirements but also from the detail design and specification phases. The feedback will need to supply the following information:

1 The technological implications for the building operation of any structural, fabric and services system implicit in the proposed building form that is evolving during the scheme designing phase. This information will have to be derived from the 'general specialist' skills/knowledge and 'general' information inputs to be used in the detail designing phase.

2 The constructional implications for building production of any structural, fabric and services systems implicit in the proposed building form that is evolving during the scheme designing phase. This information will have to be derived from the 'general specialist' skills/knowledge and 'general' information inputs to be used in the specifying phase.

3 The *actual* constructional consequences in building production of the evolved building form from the scheme designing phase. This information will have to be derived from the 'detail project' skills/ knowledge and 'specific' information used in the constructing phase.

Unless the feedback can exist for (1) and (2) above, the information and/or skills/knowledge inputs to any head task or sub-task that contain elements of *design review* will be deficient. Unless the feedback can exist for (3) above, the information and/or skills/knowledge inputs to any head task or sub-task that contain elements of *controlling changes to the design baseline* will be deficient.

Who carries out these tasks?

The project participants responsible for making inputs to each of the head tasks (and therefore any sub-task under that heading) are as follows:

B   *Final brief* – the client and the architect/designer.
B1 *Space use/material study* – the architect/designer.

B10 *Alternative solutions* – the architect/interior/structural/services designers and the client.

B11 *Location drawing set* – the architect/interior/structural/services designers.

B12 *Validated scheme design* – the architect/interior/structural/services designers, the manager, the specialist contractor designer(s) and the client.

B13 *Final scheme design* – the architect/designer.

Unless these participants make a responsible contribution to the above tasks as allocated, the skills/knowledge inputs will all be deficient.

Overcoming current problem areas in this phase

The particular problems in current practice that have to be overcome to eliminate input deficiencies in the tasks of the scheme designing phase are as follows:

1   The scheme designing phase is concerned with those aspects of the building project that are the *most* difficult to measure, and therefore defining acceptance criteria for conforming to requirements poses a severe problem; e.g. the requirements for (a) external aesthetic appearance, (b) internal ambience of spaces, (c) a 'healthy' internal environment and (d) best space arrangement and circulation are all *highly subjective* in terms of individual personal satisfaction.

2   Even if these aspects could be defined with reasonably measurable acceptance criteria, the people who will be the most concerned about whether conformance to requirements has been achieved (i.e. the end users) are not usually involved in the briefing and scheme designing phases of a building project.

3   It is likely that once the building is in operation the *original* requirements will be implicitly changed, meaning that non-conformance to requirements now occurs.

The suggested answers to these problems are the following changes to current building design practice:

○   *All* requirements which are now subjective in terms of judging satisfaction should be made objective with clearly defined acceptance criteria, and there is no reason why this cannot be achieved; e.g. it is possible to describe an aspect of architectural aesthetic appearance in terms of *dimensional proportion* requirements[44].

○   The client must take responsibility for defining the end user requirements, as he or she is the participant responsible for initiating the building project and making the judgements about the building as a product and how it should satisfy the needs of the customer in the marketplace.

○ The original requirements that were conformed to should be traceable and be supplied with the final building in operation, e.g. future computer knowledge bases that belonged to finished buildings in order to make them 'intelligent' would have to contain this information[45].

Unless these changes are implemented in current building design practice it is likely that the skills/knowledge and information inputs to the head tasks (and all sub-tasks) will continue to be deficient, with resulting defects in the outputs. It follows that the information inputs to the tasks in the subsequent detail designing and specifying phases will be deficient.

Schedule 2 below indicates each element input to each task in the scheme designing phase and, when read in conjunction with Figs. 8.1 and 8.2, will further indicate the element detail input to each element. The purpose of Schedule 2 is to guide the reader in planning to prevent deficiencies occurring in the scheme designing phase of the project. Deficiencies will be prevented if:

1 Every task is always carried out, and always in the logically defined sequence.

2 The description is always borne in mind when the task is being carried out, as this is its essential purpose.

3 The element inputs are always appropriate to the specific task in question in terms of a project management application.

4 The element detail inputs are always appropriate to and in place for the specific element in question in terms of corporate management support.

5 The output is not expected to be anything more or anything less than is stated.

If defects have occurred in this particular phase in past projects, the cause can be traced through the task to the element and finally to the element detail.

Schedule 2: Scheme designing

No. B
Description Brief for completeness
Inputs *Skills/knowledge* Detail for project/general for specialists
Performance standard 1st call 86%/2nd call 95%/3rd call 100%

	Procedure	Identify critical factors/produce checklists
	Materials	Information specific to project/ specialists
	Facilities/equipment	Information storage/retrieval/ application
Output	FINAL BRIEF	

No.	B1	
Description	Space use and relationship and appropriate materials	
Inputs	*Skills/knowledge*	Detail for project/general for specialists
	Performance standard	1st call 68%/2nd call 95%/3rd call 100%
	Procedure	Define unique factors/produce unique statement
	Materials	Information specific to project/specialists
	Facilities/equipment	Information storage/retrieval/ application
Output	SPACE USE, MATERIAL STUDY	

No.	B10	
Description	Alternative spatial solutions in order to resolve conflicts	
Inputs	*Skills/knowledge*	Detail for project/specialists
	Performance standard	Not less than 2/not more than 5 to give 100%
	Procedure	Select spatial arrangements/ structural forms
	Materials	Information specific to project/ specialists
	Facilities/equipment	Information application/ representation
Output	ALTERNATIVE SOLUTIONS	

No.	B11	
Description	Location drawings and physical models for review	
Inputs	*Skills/knowledge*	Detail for project/specialist/ general for graphics
	Performance standard	Adequacy/correctness – 100%

	Procedure	Select method/produce visual display
	Materials	Information specific to project/ specialists
	Facilities/equipment	Information representation/ presentation
Output	LOCATION DRAWING SET	

No.	B12	
Description	Scheme design against brief requirements	
Inputs	*Skills/knowledge*	Detail for project/general for specialists
	Performance standard	Adequacy – 100%
	Procedure	Compare alternatives/test against requirements
	Materials	Information specific to project/ specialists
	Facilities/equipment	Information application/ presentation
Output	VALIDATED SCHEME DESIGN	

No.	B13	
Description	Appropriate solution	
Inputs	*Skills/knowledge*	Detail for project/general for specialists
	Performance standard	Correctness – 100%
	Procedure	Select an alternative/modify to satisfy test
	Materials	Information specific to project/ specialist
	Facilities/equipment	Information retrieval/application/ representation
Output	FINAL SCHEME DESIGN	

Chapter 9

The designing phase – detail

Whereas the scheme designing phase was essentially concerned with those aspects of a building that make it aesthetically and socially acceptable, the detail designing phase is concerned with those aspects of a building that enable it to perform technically in its various parts and in support of the building's performance as a whole.

The technological systems that fail when the building is in operation concern every elemental part of the building, although it is usually the external envelope (walls, roofs and ground floors) where most problems occur, and their physical damage effects, defect causes (in design, construction or product) and possible remedies are all well documented in various government studies[17] and other[46] sources. It is also because of faults such as rain penetration, rising damp, condensation, metal corrosion, timber rot, delamination of composites, disconnection of fixings and mechanical breakdown of hardware and services systems in the building in operation that the architect/designer currently faces onerous liability claims.

It is strange, however, that the great majority of the physical damage effects of these defects occur because of well-known scientific principles (i.e. they do *not* happen because building technology is exceptionally innovative and therefore stretching the limits of scientific knowledge). It has been suggested, however, that these failures occur because each building (and its elemental parts) is a unique 'system' and therefore the failure is a system failure which results in a technological failure. It is the unique combination of material, component, element, configuration and environment – as well as people – involved in the total design, construction and operation of the building that is the cause of the defect that results in damage[47].

Detail designing is therefore concerned with the selection of structural, fabric and services technological systems to create the elements of the built form defined in scheme designing. This selection can be concerned with the selection of a single material or component to be designed into an elemental fabric system by the architect designer or the selection of a complete elemental system itself which has been designed by the specialist contractor designer (e.g. a curtain walling system). The same alternative situation applies to the structural system and structural designer and services system and services designer. Detail designs have to take into account the following factors:

1   The conditions of use of each building element according to its internal and/or external environment.

2   The chemical and physical characteristics of the material, component or system selected for the building element and element junctions.

3   The induced and inherent dimensional variability characteristics of the material, component or system selected for the building element and element junctions.

4   The on-/off-site assembly implications of the element and element junctions as they affect and are affected by items (1)–(3) above.

Detail design proposals are traditionally presented through scale drawings, models, life-size physical prototypes and supporting non-graphical data[48] for assessing requirement satisfaction and (if agreed) developing into specification for construction.

As noted in Chapter 8, standard details may be utilized (albeit with minor modifications) both in part or as a total building system for a particular scheme design. However, it should be emphasized that this practice is no guarantee of success unless rigorously reviewed for the scheme design in question.

How, then, has the model viewed this particular phase of the process? What are the critical tasks and their outputs? How can the key inputs be free of deficiencies? Who, of all the project participants, is responsible?

What are the critical tasks?

As with each phase of the model, a number of critical tasks have been identified. It is proposed that these tasks are only the heads of a set of sub-tasks beneath them, the number of which will vary from project to project and from task to task (e.g. the task B15, *Services/fittings study*, will have many sub- and even sub-sub-tasks beneath its head). The point is that only if these critical head tasks begin with the appropriate inputs is it possible for the sub-tasks beneath them to have appropriate inputs.

This, however, can only occur if the consistency and integrity of the model approach is itself carried through.

The specific critical head tasks (the name of which is their essential output) that must be carried out in order to ensure that the defined detail design solutions(s) can be demonstrated to meet the defined building requirements and the defined scheme design solution(s) are as follows:

B14   Structure/Envelope Study
B15   Services/Fittings Study
B16   Alternative Solutions
B17   Detail Drawing Set
B18   Validated Detail Design for Performance
B19   Final Detail Design

Before the nature of these tasks and their inputs through the levels of the model are examined it is necessary to see what the Quality Systems Standard[5] suggests as principles for this particular phase. The part of ISO 9004 that most mirrors the scheme and detail designing phases and the specifying phase has been described in the previous chapter.

Many of those elements can equally apply to both scheme *and* detail designing, although the *types* of requirements with which they are concerned differ considerably. This can be appreciated in such items as, for example, 'reliability, maintainability and serviceability', which can have a much more specific and detailed meaning in terms of acceptance criteria for verification for aspects of detail designing than scheme designing. For example, in scheme designing selected patterns of windows have to satisfy such criteria as aesthetic proportion and material appearance, quality of day- and sunlight into the interior, etc.[49], whereas in detail designing selected window components must satisfy such criteria as weather-resistance to a particular exposure, security of fixings and hardware, etc.

It can therefore be argued that in the detail designing phase it should become easier to undertake such things as 'defining acceptance criteria', 'measure' and 'test' for conformance to requirements because the requirements to be met in this particular phase can be far less subjective, both in their original definition and judgement for conformance. It is equally important that this is so, because the decisions made about requirements and their conformance in this particular phase determine whether, in its operation, the building will be judged to have succeeded or failed technologically.

Bearing in mind, then, all the elements of a quality management system described in Chapter 8 (which must be used if formal QA is to be obtained for the design practice) and the stated objective of the model's designing phase shown in Fig. 9.1, the element inputs to each of the tasks that comprise this particular phase can be considered in terms of the criticality of deficiencies in inputs and the likely consequences. In Fig. 9.1 it can be seen that feedback loops into this phase come from various task outputs in the specifying and constructing phases, and task outputs from this phase feed back into the briefing phase. The elements on the right-hand side are concerned with those inputs that affect how the information of requirements is both formulated and handled. This is the information that will begin to accumulate from the designer's scheme design, and will finally develop into a fully documented detail design that can be compared against the developed brief and scheme design, i.e. B14, *Structure/envelope study*, to B19, *Final detail design*.

For example, a deficiency in the project-specific information in task B14 will result in a defect in the output of the structure/envelope study, and this study in turn will become a deficient part of a number of the information inputs to subsequent tasks, which in their turn will then have a defective output.

On the other hand, a deficiency in the general information about the particular type of building element the designer had in mind (e.g. the technological characteristics of a specific type of cladding system) would also result in a defective structure/envelope study, which would then become a deficient information input to subsequent tasks because the

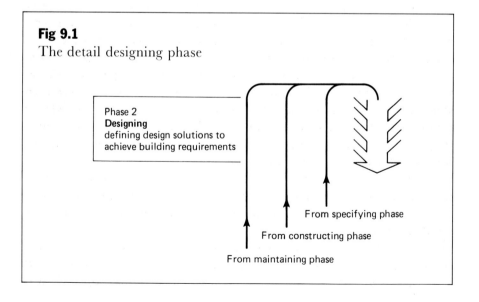

Fig 9.1
The detail designing phase

matching of the cladding system's characteristics with the scheme design's implied conditions of service could not be made.

Even though the information itself may not be deficient, the means of information technology (in terms of storage, retrieval, application, presentation and presentation) may well be. Essentially, the problem of information technology in a building project stems from the fact that many different participants – all with diverse interests in the project and ways of thinking – are involved over a comparatively long period of time. This results in the need to be able to appropriately utilize different media between participants at different times throughout the project as the information itself changes in type and detail.

The problem of information technology in the detail designing phase should become even less acute than in the scheme designing phase of a building because:

O   The architect/designer now has a fairly well-defined scheme in terms of a building design proposal which can be communicated to other designers, i.e. structural, services, interior and specialist contractor.

O   Some drawn detail design (and supporting calculations) exists, which gives all participants some basis upon which to communicate information.

O   The means of information technology to suit all likely future project participants will have started to evolve.

However, deficiencies in this particular element input will also result in a defective output to any of the designing phase tasks. For instance, in task B18, *Validated detail design for performance*, if a particular functional performance's conformance to requirements cannot be adequately presented then validation will be incomplete. Consequently, there will be a deficiency in the information input to task B19, *Final detail design*.

In Fig. 9.1 the elements on the left-hand side are concerned with the 'people' inputs in terms of their skills and knowledge, procedures (i.e. the way in which each of the different designers work) and performance standard (i.e. the appropriate level of attainment that is expected of a particular individual carrying out the task). Deficiencies in any one of these element inputs can therefore have a great variety of generic causes, some of which could be as follows:

O   A lack of either skill or knowledge (or both) by individual(s) for a particular task as a result of appointing the wrong person to carry it out (this could be especially true in this phase if new technology is implicit in the detail design).

O   A lack of an appropriate procedure as a result of following traditional professional or commercial practices which are inappropriate to the task required for a particular project. This could be especially true in this phase if specialist contractors who have knowledge of specific elements are not involved.

○ A lack of conviction in the ability to reach a particular performance standard for a specific task, due to an inherent cultural attitude of a sector of the construction industry.

In the detail designing phase, for instance, a deficiency in the knowledge input in task B17, *Detail drawing set*, will result in a defective ouput, which in turn will cause a deficient information input to task B18, *Validated detail design for performance*, the defective output of which has been described above. Another example is that a deficiency in either procedure or performance standard inputs into task B15, *Services/fittings study*, would result in an incomplete study as the output, which in turn becomes deficient information into many of the subsequent tasks in the detail designing and specification phases.

Bearing these likely causes of deficiencies in mind, the ideal element inputs to every task in the detail designing phase is shown in Schedule 3 below, and the relationship of each task to the other is outlined in Fig. 9.2.

Why controlled feedback is important

Controlled feedback loops are needed not only within the detail designing phase itself to maintain consistency in meeting requirements but also from the specifying and constructing phases. The feedback will need to supply the following information:

1 The constructional implications for building production of any of the detail selection of specific materials, components and systems and detail junctions within and between elements of the building in terms of:

  (a) The requirements for on- and/or off-site assembly.

  (b) The requirements for dimensional accuracy in on- and off-site assembly.

  (c) The requirements for the work sequence of on-site assembly. This information will have to be derived from the 'detail project' skills/knowledge and 'specific' information inputs to be used in the specifying phase.

  (d) The requirements for disassembly when the building is in operation. This information will have to be derived from the 'detail project' skills/knowledge and 'specific' information to be used in the maintaining phase, fed through the briefing and scheme designing phases.

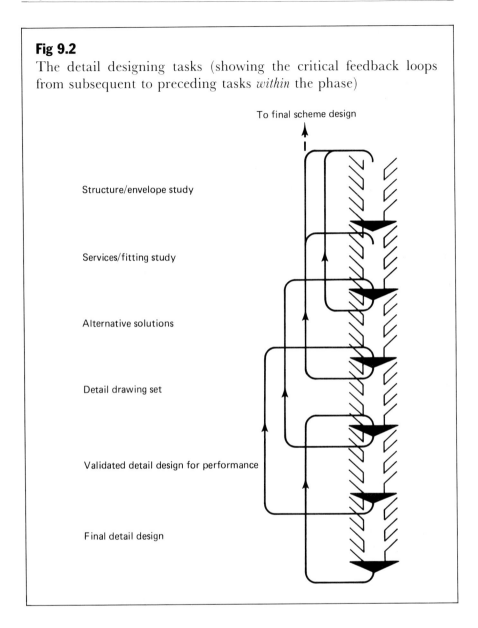

Fig 9.2
The detail designing tasks (showing the critical feedback loops
from subsequent to preceding tasks *within* the phase)

To final scheme design

Structure/envelope study

Services/fitting study

Alternative solutions

Detail drawing set

Validated detail design for performance

Final detail design

2   The actual constructional sequence in building production of the
evolved element detail design from the detail designing phase. This
information will have to be derived from the 'detail project' skills/
knowledge and 'specific' information used in the constructing phase.
    Unless the feedback can exist for (1) above, the information and/or
skills/knowledge inputs to any head task or sub-task that contains

elements of *design review* will be deficient. Unless the feedback can exist for (2) above, the information and/or skills/knowledge inputs to any head task or sub-task that contain elements of *controlling change to the design baseline* will be deficient.

Who carries out these tasks?

The project participants responsible for making inputs to each of the head tasks (and therefore any sub-task under that heading) are as follows:

B14 *Structure/envelope study* – the architect/structural/services designers and specialist contractor designers

B15 *Services/fittings study* – the architect/interior/services designers and specialist contractor designers

B16 *Alternative solutions* – the architect/interior/structural/services designers and specialist contractor designers and the client

B17 *Detail drawing sets* – the architect designer/interior/structural/ services designers and specialist contractor designers

B18 *Validated detail design for performance* – the architect designer/ interior/structural/services designers and specialist contractor designers and the client

B19 *Final detail design* – the architect designer

Unless these participants make a responsible contribution to the above tasks as allocated, the skills/knowledge inputs will all be deficient.

Overcoming current problem areas in this phase

The particular problems in current practice that have to be overcome to eliminate input deficiencies in the tasks of the detail designing phase are as follows:

1   The detail designing phase is concerned with those aspects of the building project that should be the *least* difficult to measure, and therefore defining acceptance criteria for conforming to requirements poses less of a problem than in the scheme designing phase. However, some problems still remain:

(a) Although, for example, a physical prototype test of a particular cladding system could demonstrate conformance to weathering requirements for a building project's external envelope, conformance in actual operation will still have to be deduced and predicted by simulation from the test.

(b) Although, for example, a commissioning test of a particular services system could demonstrate conformance to detection requirements for a building project's security, conformance in actual operation will still have to be deduced and predicted by simulation from the test.

2 Even if these aspects can be defined with reasonably measurable acceptance criteria by test and simulation, the people who will be most concerned whether conformance to requirements has been achieved (i.e. the end users) are not usually involved in the briefing and detail designing phases of a building project.

3 It is likely that once the building is in operation the original requirements will be implicitly changed, meaning that non-conformance to requirements now occurs.

The suggested answers to these problems are the following changes to current building design practice:

O   *All* requirements which are now objective in terms of judging satisfaction by physical prototype or commissioning test should be supported by simulation if acceptance criteria are to be credible.

O   The client must take responsibility for defining the end-user requirements, as he or she is the participant responsible for initiating the building project and making the judgements about the building as a product and how it should satisfy the needs of the customer in the marketplace.

O   The original requirements that were conformed to should be traceable and be supplied with the final building in operation, e.g. future computer knowledge bases that belonged to finished buildings in order to make them 'intelligent' would have to contain this information[45]. This would be even more applicable to those characteristics of a building determined in the detail designing phase than those in the scheme designing phase.

Unless these changes are implemented in current building design practice it is likely that the skills/knowledge and information inputs to the head tasks (and all sub-tasks) will continue to be deficient, with resulting defects in the outputs. It follows that the information inputs to the tasks in the subsequent specifying phase will be deficient.

Schedule 3 below indicates each element input to each task in the detail designing phase and, when read in conjunction with Figs 9.1 and 9.2, will further indicate the element detail input to each element. The purpose of Schedule 3 is to guide the reader in planning to prevent deficiencies occurring in the detail designing phase of the project. Deficiencies will be prevented if:

1 Every task is always carried out, and always in the logically defined sequence.
2 The description is always borne in mind when the task is being carried out as this is its essential purpose.
3 The element inputs are always appropriate to the specific task in question in terms of a project management application.
4 The element detail inputs are always appropriate to and in place for the specific element in question in terms of corporate management support.
5 The output is not expected to be anything more or anything less than is stated.

If defects have occurred in this particular phase in past projects, the cause can be traced through the task to the element and finally to the element detail.

Schedule 3: Detail designing

No.	B14	
Description	Structural system and external envelope	
Inputs	*Skills/knowledge*	Detail for project/general for specialists
	Performance standard	Adequacy – 100%
	Procedure	Define structural and envelope requirements
	Materials	Information specific to project/ specialists
	Facilities/equipment	Information storage/retrieval/ application
Output	STRUCTURE/ENVELOPE STUDY	

No.	B15	
Description	Internal sub-division, services systems, finishes and fittings	
Inputs	*Skills/knowledge*	Detail for project/general for specialists
	Performance standard	Adequacy – 100%
	Procedure	Define services and sub-division requirements
	Materials	Information specific to project/ specialists

	Facilities/equipment	Information storage/retrieval/ application
Output	SERVICES/FITTINGS STUDY	

No.	B16	
Description	Alternative detail design solutions to resolve conflicts	
Inputs	*Skills/knowledge*	Detail of project/general for specialists
	Performance standard	Not less than 2/not more than 5 to give 100%
	Procedure	Select structural systems/services systems
	Materials	Information specific to project/ specialists
	Facilities/equipment	Information representation
Output	ALTERNATIVE SOLUTIONS	

No.	B17	
Description	Component and assembly drawings and models for review	
Inputs	*Skills/knowledge*	Detail for project/general for graphics
	Performance standard	Adequacy/correctness – 100%
	Procedure	Select method/produce visual display
	Materials	Information specific to project specialists
	Facilities/equipment	Information representation/ presentation
Output	DETAIL DESIGN DRAWINGS	

No.	B18	
Description	Detail design against brief requirements	
Inputs	*Skills/knowledge*	Detail for project/general for specialists
	Performance standard	Adequacy – 100%
	Procedure	Compare alternatives/test against requirements
	Materials	Information specific to project/specialists

	Facilities/equipment	Information application/ representation
Output	VALIDATED DETAIL DESIGN	

No.	B19	
Description	Appropriate solution	
Inputs	*Skills/knowledge*	Detail for project/general for specialists
	Performance standard	Correctness – 100%
	Procedure	Select an alternative/modify to satisfy test
	Materials	Information specific to project/ specialists
	Facilities/equipment	Information retrieval/application/ representation
Output	FINAL DETAIL DESIGN	

Chapter 10

The specifying phase

The results of the research project[32] that produced the model also showed that, comparing its ideal approach in achieving a chain of conformance to requirements throughout a building project with real-world practice, specification as a phase was potentially the weakest link in the chain. The reasons for this can be deduced by considering the objective of this particular phase, i.e. defining production requirements to achieve design solutions, and what happens about specification for a building design in practice. The problem can be described as follows.

If 'specifying' is defining the production requirements of a given design solution then, by definition, those requirements must include a detailed method of assembly that can demonstrably achieve the given design solution. However, in current building design practice the designers only specify the material and workmanship – usually in rather broad and general terms – and it is left to the specialist contractors to determine the exact method. This means that current building design and practice divides the total responsibility for specification in the building project process. The result of this situation is twofold:

1   The majority of problems that occur on-site in terms of 'buildability'[50] can be traced to this division of responsibility for specifying exactly how the given design solution – for both scheme and detail – in an agreed manner before either on- or off-site assembly commences.

2   The model must assume that the specifying phase will include the exact method for production – or choice of equally proven methods – if its aim of achieving a chain of conformance to requirements throughout the building project is to be realized.

An example of the problems caused by this situation in practice – and ones that the application of this model should solve – concerns the issue of dimensional variability in construction assembly. Any given detail designed junction between components within an element or between elements will require a certain level of accuracy to be achieved in its production if it is to perform in operation as the designer intended. This particular level of accuracy can only be achieved if the characteristic dimensional variability of the specific materials and constructional forms[51] plus the specific method of production is taken into account and planned for before either off- or on-site assembly commences.

Specifying is therefore concerned with the selection of specific methods of production to physically realize the building elements and their junctions defined in detail designing. This selection may range as widely as the choice of a particular specialist contractor to provide a totally assembled system for a complete element or elements to the selection of a particular material, component or trade skill, having regard to availability at a particular time in a project. Specifications have to take into account the following factors:

1 The manpower (especially in terms of particular trade skills), materials and plant required to construct the building elements in terms of work sequence, time and cost targets.

2 The chemical and physical characteristics of the material, component or system selected for the building elements in terms of materials handling, storage and protection of site-stored materials and components or completed elements.

3 The induced and inherent dimensional variability characteristics of the material, component or system defined for the building element and element junction in terms of levels of accuracy in production.

4 The on-/off-site assembly requirements of the element and element junctions as they affect and are affected by items (1)–(3) above.

Once they have been determined, specification proposals are traditionally presented through structured written text related to detail design drawings[52], exploded work-sequence drawings, and life-size physical prototypes for assessing requirement satisfaction and – if agreed – passing to the tendering phase for construction. As with standard details, using standard specifications and general reference to British Standards is no guarantee of success unless they are rigorously reviewed for the particular situation of the scheme and detail design in question.

How, then, has the model viewed this particular phase of the process? What are the critical tasks and their outputs? How can the key inputs be free of deficiencies? Who, of all the project participants, is responsible?

What are the critical tasks?

As with each phase of the model, a number of critical tasks have been identified. It is proposed that these tasks are only the heads of a set of sub-tasks beneath them, the number of which will vary from project to project and from task to task (e.g. the task C12, *Temporary works requirements*, will have many sub- and even sub-sub-tasks beneath its head). The point is that only if these critical head tasks begin with the appropriate inputs is it possible for the sub-tasks beneath them to have appropriate inputs. This, however, can only occur if the consistency and integrity of the model approach is itself carried through.

The specific critical head tasks (the name of which is their essential output) that must be carried out to ensure that the defined scheme and detail design solutions can be demonstrated for practical construction in production requirements are as follows:

C   Constructable design
C1   Classification system
C10   Information database
C11   Contractual requirements
C12   Temporary works requirements
C13   Accuracy requirements
C14   Validated design for construction
C15   Procedural specification
C16   Technical specification
C17   Validated specification
C18   Final specification
C19   Drawing/specification set

Before the nature of these tasks and their inputs through the levels of the model are examined it is necessary to see what the Quality Systems Standard[5] suggests as principles for this particular phase. The part of ISO 9004 that most mirrors the specifying phase is that which has already been described in Chapter 8 and, in addition, those parts under the headings 'Quality in procurement' and 'Quality in production'.

Although it might be argued by current architect/designers that the latter two headings seem more appropriate for building construction than for building design, in the terms of the model, these aspects of the building project must concern the designer and must come in the specifying phase if the design solution is to be physically realized as intended.

It is interesting to note at this point that the Quality System Standard – originating from the world of manufacturing – recognizes no discontinuity in or divided responsibility for design and production in the total project process. More often than not – except in the case of design-and-build procurement – this is the opposite to the situation found in current design and construction practice; consequently, exactly relating the structure of the Standard to current practice is difficult.

The additional elements pertinent to the specifying phase under these two headings require the supplier to:

O   Plan and control purchased supplies of materials, components, assemblies, calibration services and special processes.

O   Establish a close working relationship and feedback system for continual quality improvement with each supplier.

O   Establish a programme which includes, as a minimum, the following elements:

—   Specification, drawing and purchase order requirements . . . including the *precise* identification of style and grade and inspection instructions.

—   Selection of qualified suppliers . . . including assessment/evaluation for capability/quality system through samples, similar history, test results and published experience of other users.

—   Agreement on supplier's quality assurance system or any acceptable method of supplier assurance.

—   Agreement on verification methods developed with the supplier . . . including inspection and test data and sampling methods for quality improvement.

—   Provisions for settling quality disputes . . . including routine and non-routine matters and improved communication channels.

—   Receiving inspection plans and controls . . . including levels of inspection and characteristics to be inspected, bearing in mind cost targets.

—   Receiving quality records . . . including maintaining historical data for assessing supplier performance and traceability.

Owing to the divided responsibility for design and construction in the building project process it is again necessary to make some interpretation of the above extracts from the Quality System Standard. In order to see the relevance of the above terms and requirements to the current architect/interior/structural/services designer's method of practice in the specifying phase of the model, it should be realized that the *prime* supplier referred to is the designer, who in effect is supplying the specification that will enable the design to be physically realized. The *subsequent* suppliers referred to are the product manufacturers and/or specialist contractors that are either being explicitly individually (or implicitly generically) specified in order to ensure that the detail design can be produced as intended.

It might be argued that the prime supplier in this instance, under current building project methods, is the organization that takes the role of general/management/specialist contractor or construction manager, not the designer. However, unless the designers are fully involved in these activities with the subsequent suppliers – whom they are either directly or indirectly specifying – then they can have no real assurance that what they have designed and specified can be physically realized as intended.

The responsibility for items mentioned in the Standard under the heading of 'Quality in Production' pose an even greater problem of interpretation, considering current building project practice. As it contains items that are essentially concerned with the planning for controlled production, they could still be considered under the specifying phase, bearing in mind the objectives of that particular phase. On the other hand, the items mentioned might be more appropriately placed under the tendering and constructing phases, which are considered in Chapter 11. Therefore in order not to deviate too much from what could be matched to current practice, the items referred to under this particular heading will be described in that chapter and not here. However, it should be borne in mind that these items can still be extremely relevant in the specifying phase, given its defined objective.

Bearing in mind the above elements of a quality management system (which must be used if formal QA is to be obtained for the design practice) and the stated objective of the model's specifying phase shown in Fig. 10.1, the element inputs to each of the tasks that comprise this particular phase can be considered in terms of the criticality of deficiencies in inputs and the likely consequences. In Fig. 10.1 it can be seen that feedback loops into this phase come from various task outputs in the tendering phase directly and from the constructing phase indirectly through the previous designing phase. The elements on the right-hand side are concerned with those inputs that affect how the information of requirements is both formulated and handled. This is the information that will begin to accumulate from the designer's detail design, and will finally develop into a fully documented specification which can be compared against the developed brief, scheme and detail design (i.e. going from task C, *Constructable design*, to C18, *Final specification*).

For example, a deficiency in the project-specific information in task C will result in a defect in the output of the constructable design; as this will mean that the design has not been fully considered for its constructability, this defect in turn will become a deficient part of a number of

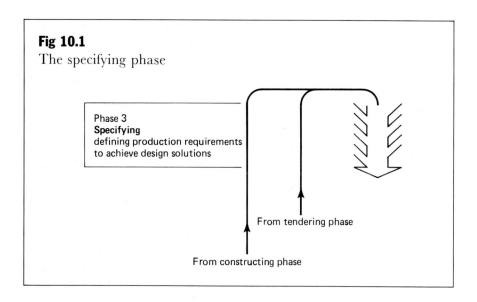

Fig 10.1
The specifying phase

Phase 3
Specifying
defining production requirements
to achieve design solutions

From tendering phase

From constructing phase

the information inputs to subsequent tasks, which in their turn will have a defective output.

On the other hand, a deficiency in the general information about the particular type of designed element junction that the designer has in mind (e.g. the dimensional variability characteristics between a steel frame and curtain walling system) would also result in a defective constructable design output which would then become a deficient information input to subsequent tasks because the matching of the dimensional variability characteristics with appropriate assembly control techniques could not be made.

Even though the information itself may not be deficient, the means of information technology (in terms of storage, retrieval, application, presentation and presentation) may well be. Essentially, the problem of information technology in a building project stems from the fact that a great number of different participants – all with diverse interests in the project and ways of thinking – are involved over a comparatively long period of time. This results in the need to be able to appropriately utilize different media between participants at different times throughout the project as the information itself changes in type and detail.

The problem of information technology should only be as acute in the specifying phase as in the detail designing phase of a building project because:

O   The architect/designer has a fairly well-defined detail in terms of the composition of and junctions between building elements which can be communicated to other designers, i.e. structural/services/interior and specialist contractor and any general/management contractor or construction manager, who must ideally be involved in this particular phase). It should be noted that the non-involvement of the latter participants is likely to cause an extreme generic skills/knowledge input deficiency in many of the tasks in this phase which could not necessarily be compensated for in information inputs on their own.

O   The majority of drawn detail design now exists, which gives all participants some basis upon which to communicate information.

O   The means of information technology to suit all likely future project participants will now be fairly well established.

However, deficiencies in this particular element input will also result in a defective output to any of the specifying phase tasks. For instance, in task C14, *Validated design for construction*, if a particular component assembly's conformance to requirements cannot be adequately presented, then validation will be incomplete. Consequently, there will be a deficiency in the information input to task C15, *Procedural specification*.

In Fig. 10.1 the elements on the left-hand side are concerned with the 'people' inputs in terms of their skills and knowledge, procedures (i.e. the way in which a particular participant works) and performance standard (i.e. the appropriate level of attainment that is expected of a particular individual carrying out the task). Deficiencies in any of these element inputs can therefore have a great variety of generic causes, some of which could be as follows:

O   A lack of either skill or knowledge (or both) by individual(s) for a particular task as a result of appointing the wrong person to carry it out.

O   A lack of an appropriate procedure as a result of following traditional professional or commercial practices which are inappropriate to the task required for a particular project.

O   A lack of conviction in the ability to reach a particular performance standard for a specific task, due to an inherent cultural attitude of a sector of the construction industry.

In the specifying phase, for instance, a deficiency in the knowledge input in task C11, *Contractual requirements*, will result in a defective output, which in turn will cause a deficient information input to task C15, *Procedural specification*, the defective output of which will cause skill and knowledge deficiencies in subsequent tasks in specifying as well as the subsequent phases of tendering and constructing. Another example is that a deficiency in either procedure or performance standard inputs into task C10, *Information database*, would result in a weak database as the output, which in turn would cause deficient information into many of the subsequent tasks in the specifying phase and subsequent tendering and constructing phases.

Bearing these likely causes of deficiencies in mind, the ideal element inputs to every task in the specifying phase is shown in Schedule 4 below, and the relationship of each task to the other is outlined in Fig. 10.2.

Why controlled feedback is important

Controlled feedback loops are needed not only within the specifying phase itself to maintain consistency in meeting requirements but also from the tendering and constructing phases. This feedback will need to supply the following information:

1 The constructional cost and time implications for building production of any of the detail and specification selection of specific materials, components and systems and detail and specification junctions within and between elements of the building in terms of:

(a) The planned production requirements for on- and/or off-site assembly;

(b) The planned production requirements for dimensional accuracy in on- and off-site assembly.

(c) The planned production requirements for the work sequence of on-site assembly. This information will have to be derived from the 'detail project' skills/knowledge and 'specific' information inputs to be used in the tendering and constructing phases.

(d) The planned production requirements for disassembly when the building is in operation. This information will have to be derived from the detail project skills/knowledge and specific information to be used in the maintaining phase, fed through the briefing and scheme designing phases.

2 The actual production constructional consequence in building production of the evolved element detail design and specification from the specifying phase. This information will have to be derived from the 'detail project' skills/knowledge and 'specific' information used in the tendering and constructing phases.

Unless the feedback can exist for (1) above, the information and/or skills/knowledge inputs to any head task or sub-task that contains elements of *design review* will be deficient. Unless the feedback can exist for (2) above, the information and/or skills/knowledge inputs to any head task or sub-task that contain elements of *controlling change to the design baseline* will be deficient.

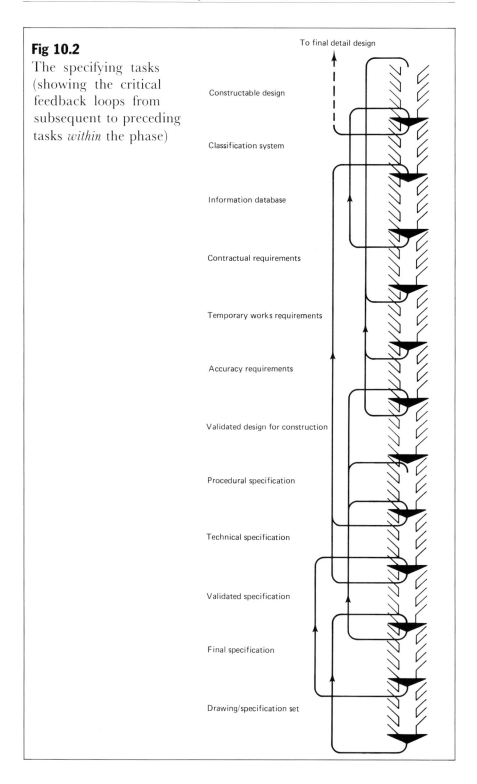

Fig 10.2

The specifying tasks
(showing the critical
feedback loops from
subsequent to preceding
tasks *within* the phase)

To final detail design

Constructable design

Classification system

Information database

Contractual requirements

Temporary works requirements

Accuracy requirements

Validated design for construction

Procedural specification

Technical specification

Validated specification

Final specification

Drawing/specification set

Who carries out these tasks?

The project participants responsible for making inputs to each of the head tasks (and therefore any sub-task under that heading) are as follows:

C   *Constructable design* – the architect/structural/services designers and specialist contractor designers and general/management contractor or construction manager
C1   *Classification system* – architect/designer and general/management contractor or construction manager
C10 *Information database* – as C1
C11 *Contractual requirements* – as C
C12 *Temporary works requirements* – as C
C13 *Accuracy requirements* – as C
C14 *Validated design for construction* – as C
C15 *Procedural specification* – as C
C16 *Technical specification* – as C
C17 *Validated specification* – the client and as C
C18 *Final specification* – the architect/structural/services/interior designers and specialist contractor designers.
C19 *Drawing/specification set* – as C18

Unless these participants make a responsible contribution to the above tasks as allocated the skills/knowledge inputs will all be deficient. It should be especially noted that not only must the general/management contractor or construction manager make contributions to the majority of tasks in this phase, but even the client must be involved in task C17 for validation.

Overcoming current problem areas in this phase

The particular problems in current practice that have to be overcome to eliminate input deficiencies in the tasks of the specifying phase are as follows:
1   The specifying phase is concerned with those aspects of the building project that will be difficult to measure, and therefore defining acceptance criteria for conforming to requirements will pose a problem unless the divided responsibility situation of current practice is overcome. Even though it might not be practical in many building projects, a

single organization cannot be totally responsible (the design-and-build procurement method being the exception) and a shared responsibility through agreed production requirements for the specifying phase must be accepted if a chain of conformance to requirements is to be achieved throughout a building project. However, some problems still remain: although, for example, a physical prototype test of the assembly (and, if necessary, the disassembly) could demonstrate conformance to a specific accuracy requirement for a particular arrangement of some specific components, conformance in actual production for all the junctions will still have to be deduced and predicted by simulation from the results of the test.

2   Even if these aspects could be defined with reasonably measurable acceptance criteria, the people who will be most concerned whether conformance to requirements can be achieved (i.e. the specialist contractor operatives) are not normally involved in the specifying phase of a building project.

3   It is likely that once the building is in production the original requirements will be implicitly changed, meaning that non-conformance to requirements now occurs.

The suggested answers to these problems are the following changes to current building design practice as follows:

○   *All* requirements which are now subjective in terms of judging satisfaction should be made objective with clearly defined acceptance criteria, and there is no reason why this cannot be achieved; e.g. it is possible to describe the finished appearance of a junction of two or more components in terms of *dimensional deviation limit* requirements[51].

○   The designers must take shared responsibilities with the producers for defining the production requirements, as both participants are interdependently responsible (and liable) for ensuring that the final building project conforms to the requirements defined in the briefing phase. The client must also take responsibility in the validation of production requirements where aesthetic appearance, functional performance and production cost/time conflicts must be resolved.

○   The original requirements that were conformed to should be traceable and be supplied with the final detail design and specification information into the production of the building and the final building in operation, e.g. future computer knowledge bases that belonged to finished buildings in order to make them 'intelligent' would have to contain this information[47].

Unless these changes are implemented in current building design practice it is likely that the skills/knowledge and information inputs to the head tasks (and all sub-tasks) will continue to be deficient, with resulting defects in the outputs. It follows that the information inputs to the tasks in the subsequent tendering and constructing phases will be deficient.

Finally, it canot be too strongly emphasized that unless the final producers of the building (i.e. the general/management/specialist con-tractors and/or construction managers) are involved, one way or another, in the specifying phase it is unlikely that a complete chain of conformance to requirements throughout the building project can be achieved.

A discontinued responsibility and (even worse) a divided knowledge base between designers and producers in this particular phase of a building project are probably the causes of the great majority of current quality-related events on-site[15] and building defects in use[17]. Therefore unless this discontinuity is prevented, there is little likelihood that total building quality can ever be realized in practice. It will be for that reason, and that reason alone, that the benefits offered by the application of a quality management system may not be realized by the construction industry and its clients at large.

Schedule 4 below indicates each element input to each task in the specifying phase of the project. The purpose of Schedule 4, read in conjunction with Figs 10.1 and 10.2, is to guide the reader in planning to prevent deficiencies occurring in the specifying phase of the project. Deficiencies will be prevented if:

1 Every task is always carried out, and always in the logically defined sequence.

2 The description is always borne in mind when the task is being carried out, as this is its essential purpose.

3 The element inputs are always appropriate to the specific task in question in terms of a project management application.

4 The element detail inputs are always appropriate to and in place for the specific element in question in terms of corporate management support.

5 The output is not expected to be anything more or anything less than is stated.

If defects have occurred in this particular phase in past projects, the cause can be traced through the task to the element and finally to the element detail. Although it might be argued by the designer that part of the responsibility for this phase – as it is defined by the model – still conventionally rests with the contractor, it is in the designer's best interests to ensure that, by whatever means, this phase is totally managed as described above.

Schedule 4: Specifying

No. C
Description Scheme and detail design for construction process
Inputs

Skills/knowledge	Detail for project/specialists
Performance standard	Adequacy – 100%
Procedure	Identify critical factors/resolve conflicts
Materials	Information specific to project/specialist
Facilities/equipment	Information retrieval/application/representation

Output CONSTRUCTION DESIGN

No. C1
Description Classification method for project specification
Inputs

Skills/knowledge	Detail for project/general for specialist
Performance standard	Correctness – 100%
Procedure	Select method/produce textual display
Materials	Information specific to project/general for specialists
Facilities/equipment	Information representation/presentation

Output CLASSIFICATION SYSTEM

No. C10
Description Appropriate sources of information
Inputs

Skills/knowledge	Detail for project/general for specialists
Performance standard	Adequacy – 100%
Procedure	Identify sources/produce unique composition
Materials	Information specific to project/general for specialists
Facilities/equipment	Information retrieval/application/representation

Output INFORMATION DATABASE

No.	C11	
Description	Contractual rules for construction process	
Inputs	*Skills/knowledge*	Detail for project specialists
	Performance standard	Adequacy – 100%
	Procedure	Define unique factors/produce unique rules
	Materials	Information specific to project/specialists
	Facilities/equipment	Information retrieval/application/representation
Output	CONTRACTUAL REQUIREMENTS	

No.	C12	
Description	Temporary works resources	
Inputs	*Skills/knowledge*	Detail for project/general for specialists
	Performance standard	Adequacy – 100%
	Procedure	Define unique factors/produce unique requirements
	Materials	Information specific to project/general for specialists
	Facilities/equipment	Information retrieval/application/representation
Output	TEMPORARY WORKS REQUIREMENTS	

No.	C13	
Description	Appropriate levels of accuracy for construction	
Inputs	*Skills/knowledge*	Detail for project/general for specialists
	Performance standard	Adequacy/correctness – 100%
	Procedure	Define unique characteristics/produce requirements
	Materials	Information specific to project/specialists
	Facilities/equipment	Information retrieval/application/representation
Output	ACCURACY REQUIREMENTS	

No.	C14
Description	Design drawings against product application requirements

Inputs	*Skills/knowledge*	Detail for project/specialists
	Performance standard	Adequacy – 100%
	Procedure	Compare design and specification/ resolve conflicts
	Materials	Information specific to project/ specialists
	Facilities/equipment	Information representation/ presentation
Output	VALIDATED DESIGN	

No.	C15	
Description	Procedural clauses for contractual requirements	
Inputs	*Skills/knowledge*	Detail for project/general for specialists
	Performance standard	Adequacy – 100%
	Procedure	Define unique factors/produce unique statement
	Materials	Information specific to project/general for specialists
	Facilities/equipment	Information retrieval/application/ representation
Output	PROCEDURAL SPECIFICATION	

No.	C16	
Description	Commodity/workmanship clauses for application requirements	
Inputs	*Skills/knowledge*	Detail for project/general for specialists
	Performance standard	Adequacy – 100%
	Procedure	Define unique factors/produce unique statement
	Materials	Information specific to project/ general for specialists
	Facilities/equipment	Information retrieval/application/ representation
Output	TECHNICAL SPECIFICATION	

No.	C17	
Description	Specification clauses against detail design requirements	
Inputs	*Skills/knowledge*	Detail for project/specialist
	Performance standard	Adequacy – 100%

	Procedure	Compare drawing and text/test against requirements
	Materials	Information specific to project/ specialists
	Facilities/equipment	Information representation/ presentation
Output	VALIDATED SPECIFICATION	

No.	C18	
Description	Appropriate specification	
Inputs	*Skills/knowledge*	Detail of project/specialists
	Performance standard	Correctness – 100%
	Procedure	Agree production requirements for building
	Materials	Information specific to project/ specialists
	Facilities/equipment	Information representation/ presentation
Output	FINAL SPECIFICATION	

No.	C19	
Description	Design drawings and specification	
Inputs	*Skills/knowledge*	Detail for project/specialists
	Performance standard	Correctness – 100%
	Procedure	Establish coordinated documentation
	Materials	Information specific to project/ specialists
	Facilities/equipment	Information representation/ presentation
Output	DRAWING/SPECIFICATION SET	

Chapter 11

The designing role in the tendering and construction phases

The role of designing during the tendering and construction phases may at first appear to be non-existent. Ideally, all design and specification has been completed and verified for its capability of being produced to the cost, time and grade targets set in the briefing phase. In an ideal world, when every task in the preceding phases has been carried out perfectly, no more designing should occur after the tendering and constructing phases have begun. However, as stated in Chapter 6, the idea of using the concept of phases instead of stages is in recognition that briefing, designing and specifying could be occurring during constructing, often for very sound and practical reasons.

Therefore in terms of progress of time, designing and specifying – as sets of tasks with distinct objectives – could be taking place during constructing; every time they do, the tendering phase will also have to occur. The essential need for a designing/specifying phase role in relation to tendering and constructing phases can be considered as follows. A design change may occur due to:

1   A change in the client's original building aesthetic/operating requirements.

2   In order to improve resource control in terms of time, cost and grade.

The reason for (1) is that, because building projects are evolving over a comparatively long period of time, a change of situation for which the building was originally briefed and designed may occur. The reason for (2) is that new information about production requirements may become available (e.g. components, methods, skills, etc.). In either case, the full set of designing/specifying tasks must be carried out as well as that of tendering tasks because the design change can have a price implication.

Although it is not the intention in this chapter to consider all the tasks involved in tendering and constructing in any great detail (all the inputs have to draw upon skills, knowledge, procedures and information not in the designer's domain), the nature of these two phases has to be considered to a level relevant to the designing and specifying roles. Tendering is therefore concerned with referring to historic and current cost data in order to determine a price for meeting the production requirements defined by the specification for achieving the proposed building design solution. These costs will, in turn, be determined by the price demanded for the specialist skills, components and materials, plant and all other management and facility support required to achieve the physical realization of the proposed building design. Tenders have to take into account the following factors:

1   The price of the specialist contractor's contribution in terms of supply and installation of a specific building element.

2   The price of any materials, components or systems to be installed by the general/management contractor or construction manager.

3   The price of all necessary temporary works, support facilities and legal/insurance costs involved in the construction process.

4   The price for the management of (1)-(3) above.

Once they have been determined, tender proposals are traditionally presented by priced schedules/bills and work programmes in order to compare them against the original time and cost targets set in the briefing phase. Standard methods of measuring the requirements and producing the schedules/bills have been used as a means of ensuring correct comparison[53] in the past. However, with the complexity of modern buildings, such methods are no longer adequate, as they were originally devised to measure material quantity only in a very general way, and modern building costs are now influenced by far more than the building design proposal's material content. Tendering proposals are presented in structured written alphanumeric text that can be related to the specification text and detail design drawings.

As with the standard specification, using standard methods of measurement and the general descriptions they employ is no guarantee that the resulting tendering proposals are an accurate reflection of the actual costs and desired profit for the contractors. As with specifications, unless the pricing process is rigorously reviewed for the particular situation of the scheme, detail design and specification, the tendering proposal will either be too high (resulting in the loss of the contract) or too low (resulting in loss of profit or an attempted lowering in the specified grade).

How, then, has the model viewed this particular phase of the process? What are the critical tasks and their outputs? How can the key inputs be free of deficiencies? Where, in particular, does the designer have a responsibility?

What are the critical tasks in tendering?

As with each phase of the model, a number of critical tasks have been identified and these can be considered as head tasks under which there could be many sub-tasks. The tasks in the tendering phase that must be carried out by others than the designers are as follows:

D	Request for proposal
D1	Capability report
D10	Resource list
D11	Specialist list
D12	Specialist tenders
D13	Costing database
D14	Priced tender
D15	Quality plan

Before the nature of these tasks and their inputs through the levels of the model are examined it is necessary to see what the Quality Systems Standard [5] suggests as principles for this particular phase. The parts of ISO 9004 that most mirror the tendering phase in building cost are under the headings 'Economics – quality-related cost considerations' (which requires the supplier to establish the basis for identifying and measuring quality-related costs in terms of operating quality costs and external quality assurance costs) and 'Quality in procurement', the elements of which have been described in Chapter 10.

1 *Operating costs* are those incurred to ensure specified quality levels, which include (a) *prevention costs* of efforts to prevent failures, (b) *appraisal costs* of testing, inspection and examination to assess whether specified quality level is being maintained and (c) *failure costs* resulting from failure before delivery (i.e. re-work) and after delivery (i.e. liability claims).

2 *External assurance costs* are those related to project-specific objective demonstration and proof required by customers.

As with the specifying phase, the divided responsibility for design and construction in the building project process makes it necessary to make some interpretation and comment on the above extracts from the Quality System Standard. In order to see the relevance of these terms and requirements to the current architect/interior/structural/services designer's method of practice in the tendering phase of the model it should be realized that:

O   The prime supplier referred to in this instance is the contractor responsible for either the whole or any part of the construction who, in effect, is supplying the physical realization of the designer's specification.

O   The subsequent suppliers referred to under 'Quality in procurement' are those who supply specialist materials, components and assemblies, which in turn may have been previously specified by the designer.

O   The 'customer' referred to above could be the client or the designer, as the latter obviously has an interest in the demonstration of how the specification requirements for the design have been met as a physical reality.

As with specifying, the fact that design and construction are separate responsibilities (and especially the fact the building projects are one-offs) creates difficulties in seeing the immediate relation of economics/quality-related costs considerations to the building project process, and especially how its requirements relate to role of the separate designer. However, some key interpretations can be made as follows:

1   Part of the cost of any tender proposal must reflect a supervision element over material component or assembly procurement and final site installation to ensure that what has been specified in design is actually physically realized. It will be more economical (and more effective in realizing design intentions) if that cost is directed towards prevention rather than all but the essential appraisal.

2   Part of the cost in any tender proposal must reflect project-specific external assurance costs where objective demonstration and proof to either the client or designer are required by the contractor in meeting *particular* project requirements.

It is in the designer's interest in knowing how the contractor intends to expend cost in terms of (1), and it is the designer's duty to clearly specify the requirements of (2). Both can and should be carried out by the designer, regardless of whether design and construction is, or is not, the single responsibility of one organization.

Bearing in mind the above elements of a quality management system (which must be used if formal QA is to be obtained for a design practice) and the stated objective of the model's tendering phase shown in Fig.11.1, the element inputs to each of the tasks that comprise this particular phase can be considered in terms of the criticality of deficiencies in inputs and the likely consequences. In Fig.11.1 it can be seen that feedback loops into this phase come indirectly from the various task outputs in the constructing phase through the previous designing

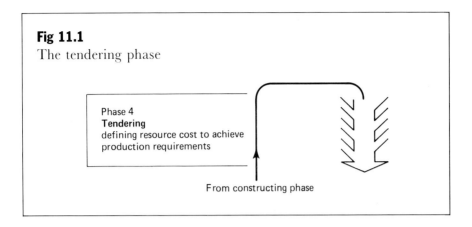

Fig 11.1
The tendering phase

Phase 4
Tendering
defining resource cost to achieve
production requirements

From constructing phase

and specifying phases. As all inputs to every task in this phase are the sole concern of the contractor, the designer can make no direct contribution to any of them. Neither can it be argued that a lack of information during this phase is the fault of the designer, as it is the contractor's responsibility to ensure that the information derived from the specifying phase is sufficient to carry out the tendering phase without any information deficiencies.

However, as it is in the designer's best interests to keep a watching brief over the contractor's tendering process, the ideal element input to every task in the tendering phase is shown in Schedule 5 below, and the relationship of each task to each other is outlined in Fig.11.2.

Constructing, the penultimate phase of a building project, is concerned with the physical realization of the outcome of the preceding designing and specifying phases, which in turn have been the translation of the client's requirements as defined in the briefing phase. As a process, constructing is also concerned with ensuring that no more costs are incurred than has been predicted as an outcome of the tendering phase.

Recent research[15] also suggests that constructing is the phase in which all the defects in the previous phases come to light. It has also been estimated that the costs incurred in this phase, because of preceding phase defects, are far greater than those incurred in the maintaining phase in terms of latent building defects.

In order to achieve its stated objective in the model the practice of constructing has to take account of the following factors:
1 The planning and control of specialist contractor contribution in terms of their production design and off-/on-site assembly of elements.
2 The planning and control of specialist supplier contribution of materials, components and plant.

Fig 11.2

The tendering tasks (showing the critical feedback loops from subsequent to preceding tasks *within* the phase)

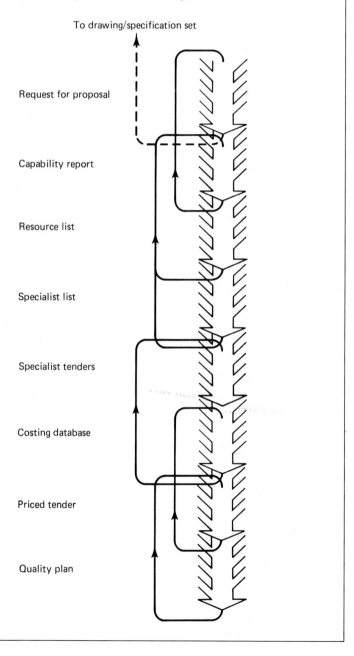

To drawing/specification set

Request for proposal

Capability report

Resource list

Specialist list

Specialist tenders

Costing database

Priced tender

Quality plan

3 The planning and control of the site in terms of plant, temporary works, materials movement and storage, protection of finished elements, amenities, and legal requirements for it to serve as a facility for production.

4 The continuous interpretation of the given design and specification for production with regard to (1)-(3) above.

Once they have been determined, constructing planning and control proposals are traditionally presented through structured alphanumeric work programmes and schedules, continuously updated as appropriate, in order to compare them against the original tendering proposals and as an aid to managing the constructing process. Standard methods of programming the constructing phase, although useful in updating and making comparisons, are no guarantee that the actual process will match the predicted process.

How, then, has the model viewed this particular phase of the process? What are the critical tasks and their outputs? How can the key inputs be free of deficiencies? Where, in particular, does the designer have a responsibility?

What are the critical tasks in constructing?

As with each phase of the model, a number of critical tasks have been identified and these again can be considered as head tasks under which there could be many sub-tasks. It is important to appreciate that in the construction phase the tasks are concerned with the overall management and not the detailed physical realization of the named output. The tasks that must be carried out by others than the designers are as follows:

E   Contract management team
E1   Contract management tool
E10   Specialist awareness
E11   Specialist appointment
E12   Accessible site
E13   Timely purchase orders
E14   Early resource order
E15   Key supervisors and operatives
E16   Credit facilities
E17   Equipment source
E18   Serviced Site
E19   Secure Storage
E20   Site layout

E21   Drained site
E22   Roads and services
E23   Supported excavations
E24   Foundations
E25   Ground slab
E26   Superstructure
E27   Floors and staircase
E28   Roof structure
E29   Exterior cladding
E30   Finished roof
E31   Partitioned spaces
E32   First fixings for services
E33   Walls and ceilings
E34   Second fixings for services
E35   Finished floor
E36   Finished decoration
E37   Finished landscape
E38   Finished building
E39   Accepted building

Before the nature of these tasks and their inputs through the levels of the model are examined it is necessary to see what the Quality Systems Standard[5] suggests as principles for this particular phase. The parts of ISO 9004 that most mirror the constructing phase in building production are under the headings of 'Quality in production', 'Control of production', 'Product cerification' and 'Control of measuring and test equipment', which require the supplier to:

○   Ensure that production operations are planned so that they proceed under controlled conditions in the specified manner and sequence. This planned control should be in terms of:

— Appropriate conditions and acceptance criteria in documented work instructions for materials, equipment, personnel, etc.

— Verification of process and product at appropriate stages with maintainance of documented test and inspection procedures.

— Process and environment capability appropriate to meeting specified requirements.

○   Ensure that production operations are controlled to be carried out as planned in terms of:

— Material control and traceability, equipment control and maintenance for key product quality characteristics.

— Special processes for equipment accuracy, operative skill, special environments and certified records.
— Process change control verification and documentation and control of non-conforming materials.
○ Ensure that end-products are verified during and at the end of the process in terms of:
— Appropriate in-process inspection and test by set-ups, operatives, automatic, fixed and patrolling for specified operations.
— Appropriate final product against specification through lot or continuous sampling.
○ Ensure that all measuring and test equipment is controlled in terms of robustness, calibration, adjustment, corrective action and all with documentation.

Although it is far easier to see how these extracts apply to the constructing phase (even when design and construction responsibility is separated) than to the preceding phases, it is still necessary to make some interpretation on the above extracts from the Quality System Standard. In order to see the relevance of these terms and requirements to the current architect/interior/structural/services designer's method of practice in the constructing phase of the model, it should be realized that the *prime* supplier referred to in this instance is the contractor responsible for either the whole or any part of the construction who is supplying the physical realization of the designer's specification. The implied customer is, in a sense, both the client (who is to receive the final end-product of the building) and the designer (who needs to be assured that the design has been constructed according to the specification).

This 'double' customer for the contractor again makes it difficult for the separate design and construction responsibility in building to be directly compared to the situation for which the Quality System Standard was devised. However, some key interpretations can be made as follows:

1 Part of the traditional professional duty of any separate designer is to ensure (as far as it is reasonable to do so) that the contractor carries out the construction according to the design specification. It is also in his best interest to do so if the design is to ultimately perform and appear as intended. A close involvement by the designer with, but not responsibility for, how the contractor *plans to control* the constructing phase (rather than waiting to see the end-products at various stages) is a more positive and cost-effective way of ensuring that design specification requirements can and will be met.

2 It has to be accepted that brief, design and specification changes will occur for one reason or another during the construction stage of a

building project. This fact is taken into account by both the Quality System Standard (which demands a positive means of change control) and the model (which recognizes phases, rather than stages, so that all ideally preceding phases can still occur in ideally subsequent phases, i.e. designing, as a set of tasks, can still be taking place during constructing). A close involvement by the designer with, but not responsibility for, how the contractor *controls* the constructing phase is essential in order to:

— Verify design if design specification is changed to achieve new production requirements because of a change in the original briefing or constructing phase objectives.
— Collect feedback on design specification in terms of its production implications for equipment, skills, etc.
— Coordinate and verify evolving specialist contractors' design into whole building design.

Only by this close involvement of design with construction as processes (both during the particular project and generally) can improvement in building as a total product be attained.

Bearing in mind the above elements of a quality management system (which must be used if formal QA is to be obtained for a design practice), and the stated objective of the model's constructing phase shown in Fig.11.3, the element inputs to each of the tasks that comprise this particular phase can be considered in terms of the criticality of deficiencies in inputs and the likely consequences. In Fig.11.3 it can be seen that feedback loops into this phase come indirectly from the various task outputs of all preceding phases. As all inputs to every task in this phase are the sole concern of the contractor, the designer can make no direct contribution to any of them. Neither can it be argued that a lack of information during this phase is the fault of the designer, as it is the

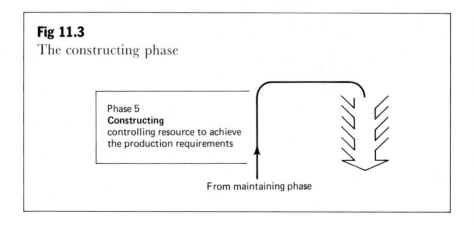

Fig 11.3
The constructing phase

Phase 5
Constructing
controlling resource to achieve
the production requirements

From maintaining phase

contractor's responsibility to ensure that the information derived from the specifying phase (as well as his own tendering phase) is sufficient to carry out the constructing phase without any information deficiencies.

However, as it is in the designer's best interests, as well as part of his professional duty, to be closely involved with the contractor's constructing process, the ideal element inputs to every task in the constructing phase are shown in Schedule 6 below and the relationship of each task to each other is outlined in Fig.11.4.

Why controlled feedback is important

Quality improvement can only come in any production process through the consistent record of how and why what was intended in design created problems in production and ultimately with the customer's use of that product.

The situation in the current process of producing a building, however, tends to militate against a continuous feedback to the designing process from the constructing and maintaining phases because of the adversarial legal position that exists between the participants responsible for each phase (i.e. the designer, the contractor and the client). This is because any admission by the first participant that design could have been improved (either for production or performance in use) would probably lead to claims for negligence from the other two participants. It is also difficult to imagine a client admitting that his initial briefing instructions could have been improved, or the contractor admitting that he could have carried out the construction at a lower cost and in a shorter time! However, ways must be found of setting up rigorous feedback between the processes of these phases, not only in-house for each participant's own organization but also between each participant responsible for these three main phases.

From the designer's point of view it is imperative that he remains fully involved in the construction process and is also willing to take a greater interest in the maintaining/managing process of finished buildings. This can only occur if, while he still remains a separate professional, such feedback can be carried out in a structured and litigation-free way in cooperation with the contractor and client. The only other possibility is to establish a single point of responsibility for both design and construction, possibly even extending to maintenance. In this situation, no legal boundaries would exist between both (or even all three) phases, and information could flow freely in feedback.

Although some architectural practices will take on the construction phase in terms of overall management, as yet they ensure that their

Fig 11.4
The construction tasks
(showing the critical
feedback loops from
subsequent to preceding
tasks *within* the phase)

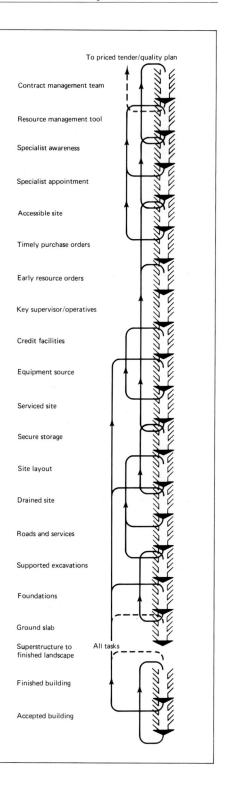

To priced tender/quality plan

Contract management team

Resource management tool

Specialist awareness

Specialist appointment

Accessible site

Timely purchase orders

Early resource orders

Key supervisor/operatives

Credit facilities

Equipment source

Serviced site

Secure storage

Site layout

Drained site

Roads and services

Supported excavations

Foundations

Ground slab

Superstructure to   All tasks
finished landscape

Finished building

Accepted building

quality management system only covers construction monitoring[54]. However, in each situation an opportunity exists for structured feedback from the construction phase to the designing and specifying phases of the project.

Who carries out these tasks?

Both the tendering and constructing phase tasks are carried out entirely by the contractor. Even if a single point of responsibility does exist, the designer makes no direct input to any of them. However, it is essential that the designer maintains a close involvement in applying a quality management system to his own design processes.

Schedules 5 and 6 below indicate each element input to each task in the tendering and construction phases. The purpose of Schedules 5 and 6, read in conjunction with Figs 11.1/11.2 and 11.3/11.4, is to guide the reader in planning to prevent deficiences occurring in the tendering and constructing phases of the project. Deficiencies will be prevented if:

1   Every task is always carried out and always in the logically defined sequence.

2   The description is always borne in mind when the task is being carried out, as this is its essential purpose.

3   The element inputs are always appropriate to the specific task in question in terms of a project management application.

4   The element detail inputs are always appropriate to and in place for the specific element in question in terms of corporate management support.

5   The output is not expected to be anything more or anything less than is stated.

If defects have occurred in this particular phase in past projects, the cause can be traced through the task to the element and finally to the element detail. Although it may be argued by the designer that the responsibility for both phases lies entirely with the contractor, specialist contractor or contruction manager, it is in the designer's best interest to ensure that, by whatever means, this phase is totally managed as described above.

Schedule 5: Tendering

No.	D	
Description	Request for proposal (RFP) for completeness	
Inputs	*Skills/knowledge*	Detail for project/general for specialists
	Performance standard	Adequacy – 100%
	Procedure	Identity critical factors/produce checklist
	Materials	Information on similar projects/specialists
	Facilities/equipment	Information storage/retrieval/application
Output	COMPLETE RFP	

No.	D1	
Description	Corporate strengths and weaknesses related to the contract	
Inputs	*Skills/knowledge*	Detail for project/general for company
	Performance standard	Adequacy – 100%
	Procedure	Identify critical factors/produce checklist
	Materials	Information specific to project/general for company
	Facilities/equipment	Information storage/retrieval/application
Output	CAPABILITY REPORT	

No.	D10	
Description	Material and human resources to meet contract	
Inputs	*Skills/knowledge*	Detail for project/specialists
	Performance standard	Correctness – 100%
	Procedure	Define unique factors/produce unique statement
	Materials	Information specific to project/company
	Facilities/equipment	Information retrieval/application/representation
Output	RESOURCES LIST	

No.	D11
Description	Specialist sub-contractor's and supplier's assessment
Inputs	*Skills/knowledge* Detail for project/specialists
	Performance standard Completeness – 100%
	Procedure Define unique factors/produce checklist
	Materials Information specific to project/specialists
	Facilities/equipment Information retrieval/application/representation
Output	SPECIALISTS LIST

No.	D12
Description	Specialist sub-contractor's and supplier's price
Inputs	*Skills/knowledge* Detail for project/specialists
	Performance standard Correctness – 100%
	Procedure Compare alternatives/test against requirements
	Materials Information specific to project/specialists
	Facilities/equipment Information representation/presentation
Output	SPECIALISTS' TENDERS

No.	D13
Description	Probable resources costs
Inputs	*Skills/knowledge* Detail for project/specialists/company
	Performance standard Correctness – 100%
	Procedure Define unique factors/produce unique statement
	Materials Information specific to project/specialists/company
	Facilities/equipment Information retrieval/application/representation
Output	COST DATABASE

No.	D14	
Description	Possible market prices	
Inputs	*Skills/knowledge*	Detail for project/specialists/ company
	Performance standard	Correctness – 100%
	Procedure	Define unique factors/ produce unique statement
	Materials	Information specific to project/ specialists/company
	Facilities/equipment	Information representation/ presentation
Output	PRICED TENDER	

No.	D15	
Description	Procedures to meet price and contract	
Inputs	*Skills/knowledge*	Detail for project/specialists/ company
	Performance standard	Adequacy – 100%
	Procedure	Define unique factors/produce statement
	Materials	Information specific to project/ specialist/company
	Facilities/equipment	Information representation/ presentation
Output	QUALITY PLAN	

Schedule 6: Constructing

No.	E	
Description	People to meet contract and system	
Inputs	*Skills/knowledge*	Detail for project/company people
	Performance standard	Completeness – 100%
	Procedure	Select people/conditions of working
	Materials	Information specific to project/ company people

	Facilities/equipment	Information storage/retrieval/ application
Output	CONTRACT MANAGEMENT TEAM	

No.	E1	
Description	Resources to meet contract and system	
Inputs	*Skills/knowledge*	Detail for project/company
	Performance standard	Completeness – 100%
	Procedure	Define unique factors/produce unique statement
	Materials	Information specific to project/company
	Facilities/equipment	Information storage/retrieval/ application
Output	RESOURCE MANAGEMENT TOOL	

No.	E10	
Description	Specialist commitment to meet contract and system	
Inputs	*Skills/knowledge*	Detail for project/specialists
	Performance standard	Adequacy – 100%
	Procedure	Define unique factors/produce unique statement
	Materials	Information specific to project/ specialists
	Facilities/equipment	Information storage/retrieval/ application
Output	SPECIALIST AWARENESS	

No.	E11	
Description	Specialist team to meet contract and system	
Inputs	*Skills/knowledge*	Detail for project/specialists
	Performance standard	Completeness – 100%
	Procedure	Select specialist/contractual arrangements
	Materials	Information specific to project/ specialists
	Facilities/equipment	Information storage/retrieval/ application
Output	SPECIALIST APPOINTMENT	

No.	E12	
Description	Safe and clear access to site	
Inputs	*Skills/knowledge*	Detail for project/general for specialists
	Performance standard	Adequacy – 100%
	Procedure	Define unique factors/produce unique statement
	Materials	Information specific to project/ general for specialists
	Facilities/equipment	Information representation/ presentation
Output	ACCESSIBLE SITE	

No.	E13	
Description	Long delivery materials and services	
Inputs	*Skills/knowledge*	Detail for project/general for specialists
	Performance standard	Completeness/correctness – 100%
	Procedure	Define unique factors/produce unique statement
	Materials	Information specific to project/ general for specialists
	Facilities/equipment	Information storage/retrieval/ application
Output	TIMELY PURCHASE ORDERS	

No.	E14	
Description	First material and service requirements	
Inputs	*Skills/knowledge*	Detail for project/general for specialists
	Performance standard	Correctness/completeness – 100%
	Procedure	Define unique factors/produce statement
	Materials	Information specific to project/general for specialists
	Facilities/equipment	Information storage/retrieval/ application
Output	EARLY RESOURCE ORDER	

No.	E15	
Description	Training to meet contract and system	
Inputs	*Skills/knowledge*	Detail for project/specialists/company people
	Performance standard	Adequacy – 100%
	Procedure	Define unique factors/produce unique method
	Materials	Information specific to project/specialists/company
	Facilities/equipment	Information representation/presentation
Output	KEY SUPERVISOR/OPERATIVES	

No.	E16	
Description	Cash flow to meet programme	
Inputs	*Skills/knowledge*	Detail for project/general for company
	Performance standard	Adequacy – 100%
	Procedure	Define unique factors/produce unique statement
	Materials	Information specific to project/general for company
	Facilities/equipment	Information storage/retrieval/application
Output	CREDIT FACILITIES	

No.	E17	
Description	Reliable plant, tools and equipment	
Inputs	*Skills/knowledge*	Detail for project/general for specialists
	Performance standard	Completeness/correctness – 100%
	Procedure	Define unique factors/produce unique statement
	Materials	Information specific to project/general for specialists
	Facilities/equipment	Information storage/retrieval/application
Output	EQUIPMENT SOURCE	

No.   E18
Description Reliable communications and public utilities
Inputs   *Skills/knowledge*   Detail for project/general for
                                            specialists
                 Performance standard   Adequacy – 100%
                 Procedure   Define unique factors/produce
                                            unique statement
                 Materials   Information specific to project/
                                            general for specialists
                 Facilities/equipment   Information storage/retrieval/
                                            application
Output   SERVICED SITE

No.   E19
Description Security to meet system
Inputs   *Skills/knowledge*   Detail for project/general for
                                            specialists
                 Performance standard   Adequacy – 100%
                 Procedure   Define unique factors/produce
                                            unique statement
                 Materials   Information specific to project/
                                            general for specialists
                 Facilities/equipment   Information storage/retrieval/
                                            application
Output   SECURE STORAGE

No.   E20
Description Facilities to meet design and specification
Inputs   *Skills/knowledge*   Detail for project/general for
                                            specialists
                 Performance standard   Completeness/correctness – 100%
                 Procedure   Define uniqe factors/produce
                                            visual display
                 Materials   Information specific to project/
                                            general for specialists
                 Facilities/equipment   Information representation/
                                            presentation
Output   SITE LAYOUT

No.	E21	
Description	Site clearance, reduced levels and ground drainage	
Inputs	*Skills/knowledge*	Detail for project/general for specialists
	Performance standard	Adequacy – 100%
	Procedure	Define unique factors/produce visual display
	Materials	Information specific to project/general for specialists
	Facilities/equipment	Information representation/presentation
Output	DRAINED SITE	

No.	E22	
Description	Site roads and mains services	
Inputs	*Skills/knowledge*	Detail for project/general for specialists
	Performance standard	Completeness/correctness – 100%
	Procedure	Define unique factors/produce visual display
	Materials	Information specific to project/general for specialists
	Facilities/equipment	Information representation/presentation
Output	ROADS AND SERVICES	

No.	E23	
Description	Excavation for foundations	
Inputs	*Skills/knowledge*	Detail for project/general for specialists
	Performance standard	Adequacy – 100%
	Procedure	Define unique factors/produce visual display
	Materials	Information specific to project/general for specialists
	Facilities/equipment	Information representation/presentation
Output	SUPPORTED EXCAVATIONS	

No.	E24	
Description	Concrete foundations	
Inputs	*Skills/knowledge*	Detail for project/general for specialists
	Performance standard	Completeness/correctness – 100%
	Procedure	Define unique factors/produce visual display
	Materials	Information specific to project/general for specialists
	Facilities/equipment	Information representation/presentation
Output	FOUNDATIONS	

No.	E25	
Description	Concrete ground slab	
Inputs	*Skills/knowledge*	Detail for project/general for specialists
	Performance standard	Completeness/correctness – 100%
	Procedure	Define unique factors/produce visual display
	Materials	Information specific to project/general for specialists
	Facilities/equipment	Information representation/presentation
Output	GROUND SLAB	

No.	E26	
Description	Supporting frames and walls	
Inputs	*Skills/knowledge*	Detail from project/general for specialists
	Performance standard	Completeness/correctness – 100%
	Procedure	Define unique factors/produce visual display
	Materials	Information specific to project/general for specialists
	Facilities/equipment	Information representation/presentation
Output	SUPERSTRUCTURE	

No.	E27	
Description	Suspended floors and staircases	
Inputs	*Skills/knowledge*	Detail for project/general for specialists
	Performance standard	Completeness correctness – 100%
	Procedure	Define unique factors/produce visual display
	Materials	Information specific to project/general for specialists
	Facilities/equipment	Information representation/presentation
Output	FLOOR AND STAIRCASES	

No.	E28	
Description	Suspended roof structure	
Inputs	*Skills/knowledge*	Detail for project/general for specialists
	Performance standard	Completeness/correctness – 100%
	Procedure	Define unique factors/produce visual display
	Materials	Information specific to project/general for specialists
	Facilities/equipment	Information representation/presentation
Output	ROOF STRUCTURE	

No.	E29	
Description	External walls and cladding	
Inputs	*Skills/knowledge*	Detail for project/general for specialists
	Performance standard	Completeness/correctness – 100%
	Procedure	Define unique factors/produce visual display
	Materials	Information specific to project/general for specialists
	Facilities/equipment	Information representation/presentation
Output	EXTERIOR CLADDING	

No.	E30	
Description	External roof finish	
Inputs	*Skills/knowledge*	Detail for project/general for specialists
	Performance standard	Completeness/correctness – 100%
	Procedure	Define unique factors/produce visual display
	Materials	Information specific to project/general for specialists
	Facilities/equipment	Information representation/presentation
Output	FINISHED ROOF	

No.	E31	
Description	Interior space division	
Inputs	*Skills/knowledge*	Detail for project/general for specialists
	Performance standard	Completeness/correctness – 100%
	Procedure	Define unique factors/produce visual display
	Materials	Information specific to project/general for specialists
	Facilities/equipment	Information representation/presentation
Output	PARTITIONED SPACE	

No.	E32	
Description	First fix of joinery and services plant and distribution	
Inputs	*Skills/knowledge*	Detail for project/general for specialists
	Performance standard	Completeness/correctness – 100%
	Procedure	Define unique factors/produce visual display
	Materials	Information specific to project/general for specialists
	Facilities/equipment	Information representation/presentation
Output	FIRST FIXINGS	

No.	E33	
Description	Interior wall and ceiling finishes	
Inputs	*Skills/knowledge*	Detail for project/general for specialists
	Performance standard	Completeness/correctness – 100%
	Procedure	Define unique factors/produce visual display
	Materials	Information specific to project/general for specialists
	Facilities/equipment	Information representation/presentation
Output	WALLS AND CEILINGS	

No.	E34	
Description	Second fix of joinery and services terminal units	
Inputs	*Skills/knowledge*	Detail for project/general for specialists
	Performance standard	Completeness/correctness – 100%
	Procedure	Define unique factors/produce visual display
	Materials	Information specific to project/general for specialists
	Facilities/equipment	Information representation/presentation
Output	SECOND FIXINGS	

No.	E35	
Description	Interior floor finish	
Inputs	*Skills/knowledge*	Detail for project/general for specialists
	Performance standard	Completeness/correctness – 100%
	Procedure	Define unique factors/produce visual display
	Materials	Information specific to project/general for specialists
	Facilities/equipment	Information representation/presentation
Output	FINISHED FLOOR	

No.	E36	
Description	Interior decoration to walls, ceilings and joinery	
Inputs	*Skills/knowledge*	Detail for project/general for specialists
	Performance standard	Completeness/correctness – 100%
	Procedure	Define unique factors/produce visual display
	Materials	Information specific to project/ general for specialists
	Facilities/equipment	Information representation/ presentation
Output	FINISHED DECORATION	

No.	E37	
Description	External hard and soft landscape	
Inputs	*Skills/knowledge*	Detail for project/general for specialists
	Performance standard	Completeness/correctness – 100%
	Procedure	Define unique factors/produce visual display
	Materials	Information specific to project/ general for specialists
	Facilities/equipment	Information representation/ presentation
Output	FINISHED LANDSCAPE	

No.	E38	
Description	Cleaning of interior and exterior works	
Inputs	*Skills/knowledge*	Detail for project/general for specialists
	Performance standard	Completeness/correctness – 100%
	Procedure	Define unique factors/produce statement
	Materials	Information specific to project/ general for specialists
	Facilities/equipment	Information representation/ presentation
Output	FINISHED BUILDING	

No.	E39	
Description	Commissioning building for use	
Inputs	*Skills/knowledge*	Detail for project/general for specialists
	Performance standard	Completeness/correctness – 100%
	Procedure	Define unique factors/produce statement
	Materials	Information specific to project/general for specialists
	Facilities/equipment	Information representation/presentation
Output	ACCEPTED BUILDING	

Chapter 12

The importance of the correct view of quality

The essence of applying QA to the business of building design and construction lies in taking the view that it concerns the total management of the process. The approach of the design practice must be one that seeks to manage the process control of designing buildings with the aim of ensuring that everything is done right first time, *every* time, from the taking of the initial brief, developing the scheme and detail design and finally preparing the design for production by specification. Even then, it will almost be impossible to achieve the aim of 'right first time, every time' unless the final specification is agreed between those responsible for the design and those responsible for the construction of the building.

Only when the management of process control is both seen and believed to be the system for the building design process will there by any chance of realizing any assurance for building as an end product. Even then, all participants, designers and builders alike, must see the system as one that accepts and allows for continuous improvement in the building process as the client's (and, ultimately, end user's) needs and expectations will continue to rise. The risk and liability of not defining and meeting these needs and expectations become increasingly onerous due to both the American and European influence on the UK construction market.

In any design practice the logical sequence for a correct understanding of and approach to quality systems must therefore be:

1   Ensure that a management for improvement approach exists as both a corporate management aim and a project management method.

2   Ensure that the management for improvement method exists in order to effect process control for conforming to requirements continuously.

3 Ensure that documented evidence exists demonstrating that process control is being carried out continuously.

Then, and only then, can external assurance be given and received with any degree of confidence. Any attempt to try to achieve the latter *without* the understanding and approach of (1)-(3) above will only result in internal cost *disbenefit* and external *discreditation* with clients and contractors alike.

The risk of design practices – and even construction companies – hastening to obtain QA certification for external purposes and then finding that this really means a long-term commitment to internal change in order to apply system and rigour to their practice processes is very great. The result of this approach may ultimately be *disbenefit* for the practice as a corporate body, *disillusionment* for the individual members of the practice, and *discreditation* with all the practice's customers (not only the building client but all the other participants who have to work with their design output on a building project).

Achieving success with quality management in the building design practice

If the wrong approach to applying quality management to the design practice and building projects will bring about failure, what is the right approach that will lead to success? The key criteria for the successful application of quality management to a building design practice are essentially the same as for its application to any other business that provides a product or a service. These criteria can be considered to be the following series of acceptances by the practice and all its members:

1 Accepting the need for a complete cultural change in the way the practice of building design is carried out – i.e. a change of attitude towards believing that the client's building requirements can be met first time, every time, and that they can be successfully translated through design and specification for the construction process.

2 Accepting that the essential aim is for cost-effective quality management, that reducing costs and raising standards are not mutually exclusive objectives. On the contrary, they must be seen as mutually supportive on the basis that if something is *not* done right first time the result is wasted resources that must have a price (i.e. cost increase) and end products that must be repaired (i.e. lower standards).

3 Accepting that, in relation to (2), getting things right first time does not militate against the inevitable change that will occur during the design and construction phases of a building project. It should rather encourage the continual definition of design base lines against which change can be rigorously controlled.

4   Accepting that architects and engineers, as the construction industry's designers, provide the design for production of the industry's building product. The implication of this is that the architectural and engineering practice will be seen as beginning a single and continuous process in the production of a building. This view supports the concept of a single point of responsibility for a building as a product, and brings the construction industry in line with the other manufacturing industries from which the principles of quality management have been derived. This does not *automatically* mean the need for a design-and-build[20] method of procurement, although this method has a distinct advantage over others in applying quality management to its processes. The same effect could be achieved through a construction management[39] method of procurement with coordinated conditions of engagement and contracts through a quality plan (see Chapter 13).

5   Accepting the structure of the model as a basis for any project and corporate system of design process control, in order to provide for *continuous* improvement in the design practice. This is because the model provides the vital link between the project management of the design of a particular building project and the corporate management of the practice that is producing that design. Both the structure of the model and the quality plan requirements of the Standard will also provide the mechanism whereby *all* project participants' (not only the designer's) efforts are combined to provide conformance to requirements for the total building project.

6   Accepting that in any quality management system the procedural systems of control will only be of benefit if they are balanced by the 'skills/knowledge' ability and 'performance standard' commitment of the individual people involved, and the general corporate and project-specific information management support of either computer-based or manual methods.

Finally, the successful implementation of a quality management system to a design practice will not ultimately depend on the under-standing and application of the system alone. A change of attitude by *all* members of the practice – from senior partner to architectural assistant – will be the key to final success. Unless people really believe the philosophy of quality and its application to their particular job (all as described in Chapter 4), any system will be ill-received and may even demotivate currently well-motivated designers.

Training aimed at changing attitudes is therefore a vital adjunct to any awareness and system training provided for the practice members.

This training must essentially entail both alleviating the fear of individual blame when quality-related problems in projects have to be identified and the cause traced, and demonstrating the benefit to the individual of the resulting improvement to practice when the cause of the problem has been removed. It is probably this fear that inhibits meaningful and useful feedback on projects, both within the practice and between the designers and the other outside project participants. (However, it has to be accepted that this fear can be real in relation to other project participants – especially the client – because of possible litigation, and this situation can only be changed by different contractual and procurement approaches.)

Ensuring that quality principles are applied and maintained

The division of responsibility for the design and construction of a building poses real problems for the participants responsible for each of these aspects. This is because the ultimate quality of the building designer's work will be affected by the quality of the work of those responsible for the building construction. Equally, the quality of the work of the latter will be affected by the quality of the requirements set by those responsible for building design.

It is probably this divided responsibility that causes many of the arguments during a project between the designer and the constructor that must be resolved through the many variations of the JCT formal contracts, and is also a root cause of the majority of the identified quality-related events on construction sites. Divided responsibility also makes it difficult for the construction industry as a whole to understand and apply the principles of the Quality System Standard[36], which was conceived for a situation where no such division exists.

At least, the Standard provides for the situation where either there is only production and installation responsibility (i.e. ISO 9002) or there is design development, production and installation responsibility (i.e. ISO 9001). Nowhere does it provide for a design-only situation, presumably because this is never the case in other manufacturing industries. However, the independent professional design practice – architectural, engineering or multi-disciplinary – in the construction industry finds itself in a position of having a design-only responsibility. Even the supervision role of the architect or engineer during the building production process is not one of total responsibility, and now also differs in its meaning according to the architect's or engineer's conditions of engagement in terms of defined levels of inspection.

The unsatisfactory outcome of this situation with regard to disputes concerning design/construction responsibility is why clients are increasingly looking for a single point of responsibility for their building projects[14]. Because of the current confused role of the design practice in construction, a clear definition of the designer's role during the tendering/constructing phases of the building has had to be outlined very clearly in Chapter 11 to enable the principles of a quality management system to be applied to the designer in particular and the building project as a whole. Given their present divided responsibilities, designers and constructors are interdependent in their efforts to achieve quality for the total building project. So too are the designers/constructors and the client, the latter being very much part of the building design and construction process. Indeed, the client's positive role in that process (essentially as decision maker when grade/cost/time conflicts have to be resolved) has long been recognized in the RIBA Plan of Work[10] and is cited in recent studies as the key to success in commercial construction projects[55].

Therefore while a divided design and construction responsibility remains and the client wishes to have a decision-making role in the process, ensuring that quality principles are maintained throughout every phase of the building project process must be a shared task.

As the ultimate phase of that process concerns the maintaining (including managing) of the building when it finally becomes the 'aesthetic and operating facility' defined in the original briefing phase, a continuing responsibility for maintaining quality principles will then fall on the client. This is because the design solutions made and physically realized in all the previous phases will, explicitly or implicitly, generate requirements for maintaining and management of the built facility which must be conformed to if the original quality expected by all project participants is to be maintained throughout the life of that building. In other words, the fact that the client has been involved throughout the design and production process – and is directly or indirectly influencing requirements and their conformance – means that maintaining quality of the building is his concern. No amount of collateral warranties or guarantees extracted from designers or constructors can really absolve the client from that obligation, even though clients are currently making strenuous efforts to do so[55].

Future use and/or design changes once the building is in operation (and the new requirements that these changes will automatically imply) must be considered in the light of the original requirements to which the building is currently conforming. This is because any change in operation will induce a state of non-conformance to the requirements that were conformed to in the designing, specifying, tendering and constructing phases of the original building project.

There are two possible ways in which problems of divided and continuing responsibility for building quality can be solved. The first lies with the concept of the 'project quality plan', which is derived from the quality standard[5] and is illustrated by a practical example in Chapter 13. This plan describes the mechanism for the shared responsibility for conformance to requirements by all participants and evolves throughout the project process, taking account of the contribution of each participant as they become involved (e.g. consultant, specialist contractor and end user).

The second solution lies with the future application of information technology to the construction industry[28]. Project-specific knowledge bases can be formed in computers that will record not only the *product* – the building's space, size, arrangement, physical components, performance ratings, etc. – but also the *process* — how the original defined requirements were conformed to. With this type of record a kind of building intelligence should exist concerning the building's current 'conformance to requirements' status and the 'what if' implications if that status is changed.

Therefore the quality of a building becomes defined and documented objectively rather than subjectively as at present, and consequently any legal, contractual and insurance post-occupancy issues will become far easier – and less costly – to resolve[57].

Conclusions

Unique and complex corporate and individual relationships and opinions will exist over a comparatively long period of time in any building project of any size. Given this fact, it has to be accepted that the definition of quality that describes it as 'conformance to requirements' is ultimately the only one that can be managed throughout all distinct but dependent phases of a building project. This is particularly true of the designing and specifying phases, which in effect translate the requirements of briefing to the physical reality that is the outcome of the constructing phase.

The 'level of excellence' and/or 'fitness for purpose' (the popular definitions of quality) desired by each participant, especially the client, can only be achieved in the finished building if all the requirements in every phase are clearly defined and communicated and have agreed acceptance criteria between the participants. The model framework described in this book provides the basis for identifying any errors that would result in defects that must *not* occur if building quality is to be improved. The framework tests any quality management system that a design practice considers it may have, and provides an aid in relating project-specific quality problems to deficiencies in corporate practices. Only if these are changed – by *every* project participant – can quality be improved and finally achieved in building.

Chapter 13

Case study 1:
A project quality plan

Quality Management International Ltd is a UK-based consultancy guiding design practices and construction companies in the successful implementation of quality management systems. Part of this work requires the corporate quality system to be moulded to fit the specific needs of particular projects. This results in quality planning by each participant for each project.

The basis of a quality plan

The objective of any participant in any project is to continually improve the cost effectiveness of his or her corporate quality management system. Most project quality plans therefore originate from a variety of corporate quality management systems. If these systems follow the model of ISO 9004, it can be expected that a compatible approach to quality planning for the project by all the participants will occur. (Larger projects, with joint venture agreements perhaps, would refer directly to ISO 9004 as a basis for its own specially developed project quality management system.)

The derivation of the elements of a quality plan is from ISO 9004, and they are as follows:

1   The time, cost, technical performance and appearance objectives and acceptance criteria: e.g. for *time*, periods required for different project phases, including the life of particular building elements; for *cost*, the amount to spend on design, specialist construction, building in operation.

2   The specific allocation of responsibilities and authority, to be updated during the different phases of the project: e.g. *between* partici-

pants, the detail design responsibility and authority between a services engineer, consultant designer and a specialist contractor designer; *within* a participant's own organization, the named person for a particular set of tasks.

3   The specific procedures, methods and instructions to be applied for planning, executing and verifying the work of each project participant: e.g. the client's method of determining the end-user requirements for the brief; an architect/structural/services designer's method of carrying out a design review during a particular phase of the project.

4   Suitable testing, inspection, examination and audit programmes at appropriate stages: e.g. the architect/services designer's proving that a cladding or services specialist contractor's proposal had met the requirements of a performance specification for a particular element; the manager's examination and audit of a particular specialist contractor's processes in order to ensure that a specific workmanship requirement would be met.

5   A method of controlling changes and modifications as the project proceeds: e.g. when the client's requirements change during the designing of particular specialist contractor's constructing phase of a project; when the manager requires a particular design change to meet a particular construction time requirement.

6   Other measures necessary to meet specific project objectives: e.g. special training for a particular technological design and construction requirement; directories of particular specialists; compatible computer systems between participants; records and document coding.

How a quality plan can be applied to a building project

Each project participant restricts quality planning to his or her particular responsibility for a project by following their own written and approved procedure. This procedure will describe a simple pro forma approach for small or simple projects. More complex ones will require a manual comprising mainly corporate procedures. These procedures are amended and supplemented to precisely define 'who does what and how' to meet the needs of the client and his project.

An example of a framework for a typical project quality plan for the architect designer's detail design contribution related to a specialist trade contractor's contribution to a project is as follows.

Section A

This section defines the quality plan revision record in terms of:

Revision
Date
Changes
Prepared by
Approved by

This ensures that the plan is always up to date, change has been systematically controlled and it carries a clear authority.

Section B – Quality plan

1   *Distribution list*: the controlled copy number and QA representative name for the client, manager, architect, structural engineer, services engineer, quantity surveyor and trade contractor. This ensures that all participants know that all other participants are working to the same plan at the same time.

2   *Scope of work*: a list of the scope of responsibilities, interpreted from the contract documents, for the architect as detail designer and trade contractor for a particular element. This will ensure that a design responsibility that the trade contractor has is clearly defined and related to that of the architect.

3   *Specification*:the code/date, title, section and page that apply to the trade contractor's work. This should ensure that the nature of the architect's statement of requirements is clear as to its performance and/or prescriptive content.

4   *Information and drawings*: the applicability of code/date, title and revision for both drawings and all other information sources. This should ensure that all drawing, specification, design guidance, standard/ code and product manufacturer design and production information input is up to date and traceable.

5   *Trials and samples*: the type, approval date and drawing/ specification reference necessary to clarify requirements. This should ensure that agreed acceptance criteria between architect and trade contractor have been clearly established.

6   *Key personnel;*: the job titles, names and responsibilities, showing the chain of command from the managing director to those who report to the senior manager on-site (for the trade contractor) and from senior partner to those who report to the project architect (for the design practice). This should ensure that 'who is responsible for what' is known to each of the project participants with regard to each participant's corporate management structure.

7   *Responsibilities*: the job titles for quality planning, quality system, audits, site (or drawing board) inspection, contract (or design commission) quality and any other aspect critical to the specific project. This should ensure that 'who is responsible, and what they are responsible for in detail' is known to each of the project participants with regard to each participant's project management structure.

8   *Inspection and test plan*: the section/item, when, by whom, and record for detail design proposal (see Chapter 20) and trade contractor's final assembly. This should ensure that expected types and times of inspection are known and related back to (5) *Trials and samples*.

9   *Method statements and checklists*: the title/activity, code and revision; this will apply equally to the architect's detail design as to the trade contractor's assembly process of the element. This should ensure that both design and construction activities are carefully planned and their methods agreed and approved before the activities are undertaken.

10   *Storage and protection*: major materials and susceptible works on the project, related to procedures for safer storage, protection and damage reports. Although this essentially refers to site, its implications can also be appreciated for drawings in the design office. This should ensure that appropriate care is taken in the evolution of the design and production of the various building elements.

11   *Non-conformance and change control*: description of non-conformance or change, corrective action commitment, designer approval for concession or repair (in production) and client approval for design change (in design), follow-up and close-out; it should describe the responsibility, procedure and forms for these activities. This should ensure that non-conformance and change – for whatever reason – is admitted and systematically controlled.

12   *Measuring and test equipment*: the type, code, how calibrated/ maintained through unique identification of items and calibration schedules. This essentially applies to site production but could also apply to design office equipment and facilities especially when computer-based systems are being used. This should ensure that non-conformance to requirements through equipment and facility faults is prevented.

13   *Records*: the type, where stored and duration, including those generated by the quality plan and the plan itself; this will apply equally to design office and site production control. This should ensure that design and process production decisions that have resulted in the end-product are all traceable.

14   *Certificates of conformity*: item, unique reference and sample signature, and the total list of items for which they will be issued and the person authorized to issue them; again, this will apply equally to the design office as to site production. This should ensure that conformance to requirements has been agreed and is demonstrable.

15   *Special training*: activity, course date and attendance/conference records for unique or new activities specifically required by the project; again, this will apply equally to the design office as to site production. This should ensure that the appropriate skills and knowledge are available as inputs to all design and production activity tasks.

16   *Special measurements*: aspect, procedure and records for special measurement/monitoring for interface with other trades. This will be expressed as 'critical dimensions' in the design process for taking account of dimensional variability and dominant dimensions in the assembly of components into elements. This should ensure that the designer and producer of a particular building element will have communicated about the critical aspects of that element's form.

Initiating and maintaining the quality plan

The client or his representative, who could be the first adviser he appoints (i.e. any of the designers or the manager), should provide the overall framework for the client's project quality plan and its upkeep from the inception of the project. Each participant – which includes the interior structural and services designers as well as the specialist contractors – can then concentrate on developing their own quality plan for controlling their unique contribution to the project. This will clarify the lateral relationships between all participants on whom they rely and who rely on them for information in order to meet the client's requirements cost-effectively. These plans are reviewed, approved and distributed in a controlled manner to ensure the means for updating and the updates themselves are communicated. Contracts tend to militate against this concept because they are fixed and adverserial by nature.

The effect of the quality plan on existing contracts and conditions of engagement

The general conditions of the most commonly used forms of contract specify responsibilities between the buyer and the seller of a building's design and construction, but they do not in themselves engender working relationships that are conducive to quality. The exchange of information necessary for getting it right first time, reducing avoidable costs and implementing timely corrective action is stifled by their adversarial stance.

Current building contractual practice has degenerated into an arrangement where the contract comprises general conditions plus bills plus drawings; the general conditions require constant interpretation to suit the particular circumstances of the project (and each of the participants), and the specification has become divorced from the design in the drawings and absorbed in the payment provisions document (i.e. the bills of quantities).

The application of quality management systems to a building project can create an arrangement where the contract comprises *general conditions* plus *special conditions* plus *payment provisions* plus *specification (materials and workmanship)* plus *drawings*; the special conditions are spelt out in the project quality plan, the payment provisions are the *only* concern of the bills, and the specification is integrated with the design represented in the drawings.

Special conditions can obviate this 'articles of war' mentality if they require *each* participant to plan (and to work to that plan) to meet the client's requirements. The project quality plan (which comprises a set of *all* participants' quality plans) is, in effect, these special conditions and should provide tangible evidence of how the client's requirements are continuously met from the inception of the project. Quality planning therefore reinforces what the *common* objective should be of *all* participants on the project: 'to meet *agreed* requirements'.

Only the client – or his representative – can require a unified and coordinated approach to project quality planning through the special conditions of engagement with designers and managers and contracts with general/management and specialist contractors. As the project's chief executive, the client or representative leads in the quality plan by providing the initial example instead of relying on the general conditions of the contract.

Conclusion

The project quality plan does not therefore make the conditions of appointment of the designer or the construction contract more legally onerous – which would *add* to the cost – but rather requires clearer and less contentious contract conditions – which should encourage a *reduction* in the cost of the project as a result of improved communications. Current forms of contract general conditions do not automatically support this clarification. However, the British Property Federation System[8] provides for and demands many of the clarifications (including the 'chief executive' concept through its client representative) required in a project quality plan.

Remember, parties only go for arbitration or court actions when both think they can win! More clearly defined responsibilities and requirements lead to less risk, better quality and lower costs.

(This example of a project quality plan framework is based on a document produced by the Construction Division of Quality Management International Ltd for a client engaged on a major building project. From an interview with and information provided by John R. Broomfield, MSc, FIQA, ACIArb, Director (Construction), Quality Management International – September 1989.)

Chapter 14

Case study 2: Public authority

The PSA Design Standards Office was the first building design practice in the UK to register as a Firm of Assessed Capability under the British Standards Institution's Registered Firms Scheme to BS 5750 Part 1: 1987.

How does the practice/organization contribute to the building project?

The Design Standards Office provides a multi-disciplinary building design and/or project management service to a variety of UK government departments for a wide range of building types. It can supply a spectrum of services, from a complete design and specification being carried out in-house, through concept design being carried out in-house and the remaining detail design and specification by outside consultants, to all the design services (even total design and construct services) being procured from outside consultants and companies. It therefore contributes to the building project as a designer, or represents the particular department client with its project management service.

Why is it implementing a quality management system?

The Design Standards Office first embarked on its quality management system as an example to its own outside design consultants and the construction industry in general as a response to a Department of Trade and Industry initiative in the National Quality Campaign. It followed from this initiative that quality improvement in building in the UK should begin with the government's building stock and therefore in the practice of designers (and, later, contractors) who produced them. Although, at first, the Design Standards Office's clients (i.e. government departments) did not require formal quality management systems for their projects, this demand has now started to arise, notably from the defence departments. This trend is likely to increase as more government departments use quality management internally as clients.

The Design Standards Office's motivation for implementing quality management was therefore for internal improvement in managing its own in-house design service; the design services provided to it by outside consultants; and the design and construction service provided for its clients from outside companies.

What difference is the system making to organizational practice?

A number of benefits are perceived as a result of the implementing of the quality management system, and they are described under the model phase inputs as follows.

People (task – skills/knowledge)

The clear description of responsibilities, support for initial training, auditing of procedures and design reviews demanded by the system all appear to help staff motivation. In the case of design reviews, these are welcomed by designers and do not militate against their creativity.

Methods (task – procedure)

The review and auditing demanded by the system has resulted in improved detail design and production drawing checking, and general awareness of their importance in the process. Change control procedures are seen as an important improvement, with documented agreement between the designer and client on the cost and time implications of briefing and designing variations.

Environment (task – performance standard)

All the demands of the system mean that senior management must have a greater involvement in projects, and thus their experience is not being lost to these projects, as tended to happen previously. The fact that the same management system is now being applied in different parts of the organization means that there is a familiarization benefit when staff have to move around to compensate for current staff-shortage problems. The existence of the management system (and the logical outcome that ouside consultants and contractors should also have a compatible system) means that controlling the service provided by these consultants and contractors can be more positive and demanding.

Materials (task – information)

The Design Standards Office Library is now providing a project-specific information service through appropriate literature searches of world-wide databases, with librarians auditing project information systems and contributing to the project work.

Equipment (task – information technology)

The Design Standards Office's information system is now continually reviewed and audited for ensuring that it is always up to date, and individual *ad hoc* systems no longer exist. There is now a far more systematic approach to information storage and retrieval, and other divisions in the PSA now take the Design Standards Office system as an example.

In general, although it is accepted that measurable benefits of applying the quality management system may take some time to be revealed, there is already some evidence that a number of costly variations that occur in the construction stage of projects is starting to decrease. A less measurable benefit is the fact tht the demands of the system are causing both internal and external management to be carried out more effectively; in the words of one of the senior managers, 'it provides us with a licence to manage'.

How is the concept of the quality plan being understood and applied?

The Design Standards Office has developed a formal framework for its own quality plan for every project it undertakes. The essential elements of that plan come under the following headings (Elements 1 to 10 concern the Project's General Information and Commission Review):

1   Brief history of project *before* its acceptance by the Design Standards Office.
2   Client organization (location and identification).
3   Means of communicating with client concerning:
    (a)   Brief.
    (b)   Approvals.
    (c)   Programme.
    (d)   Client-supplied material.
    (e)   Client specialists.

4 Client representatives (name, address, telephone number and date appointed):
  (a) PSA secretariat.
  (b) Client user.
  (c) Client HQ (project sponsor).
  (d) Other.

5 Other relevant Authorities not required for Commission Review (name, address and telephone number):
  (a) PSA UKTO Director.
  (b) PSA District Works Officer.
  (c) District planning authority.
  (d) Electricity.
  (e) Gas.
  (f) Water.
  (g) Telephone.
  (h) Other.

6 Project team members (name, address, telephone number and date appointed):
  (a) Group manager.
  (b) Project manager.
  (c) Design team leader.
  (d) Project architect.
  (e) Civil/structural engineer.
  (f) Public health engineer.
  (g) Mechanical and electrical engineer.
  (h) Quantity surveyor.
  (j) LS architect.
  (k) Estate surveyor.
  (l) Allocation of special duties.

7 The project:
  (a) Description.
  (b) Brief (all briefing documents and list of additional information and date deadline, before accepting the commission).

8 Programme and resources:
  (a) General programme.
  (b) Detailed programme for Stage 1.0: feasibility study, team meetings, information interchange between disciplines, reviews and consultations with internal/external specialists/authorities.
  (c) Resources: staff, consultants, agencies and other services, making allowance for holiday, time work charge (fees), etc.

9 Special services, studies or facilities: surveys, models, prototypes, structural analyses, design or materials investigation, and if within or outside scale fees.

10 Commission review, resulting in acceptance or rejection:
(a) If rejected, the recommended action for feasibility study, brief development, programme revisions, research programme.
(b) If accepted, completion of element 12, Gate to Stage 2.1 (outline scheme design) for design projects, and Element 11, Stage 1.0, for feasibility study. Acceptance is authorized by a director.

11 Completion to Stage 1.0:
(a) All studies complete as Element 9.
(b) Feasibility brochure complete.
(c) Date for client approval agreed.
(d) Approval to submit to client, with confirmation that the quality plan has been reviewed and all actions complete. Approval is given by group manager and director.

12 Gate to Stage 2.1 (outline scheme design):
(a) Feasibility study approved by the client.
(b) Brief agreed and recorded as Element 7.
(c) General programme agreed as Element 8 and any recorded changes in programme *since* commission review.
(d) Approval to proceed to next stage, with confirmation that the quality plan has been reviewed and all actions complete. Approval is given by group manager and director.

The quality plan now addresses the different sequential stages in the PSA plan of work.

Stage 2.1 (Outline scheme design)

1 Programme and resources:
(a) General programme: *either* updated Stage 1 programme with confirmed concessions *or* new programme if substantial delay awaiting approval or no feasibility study.
(b) Detailed programme for current Stage 2.1 (outline scheme design): dates for design team meetings, formal exchange between disciplines, completion of studies/investigations, design reviews, presentations to client, etc.
(c) Programme concessions from previous Stage 1 if programme differs from Stage 1, Element 8.
(d) Resources: internal staff, consultants to be commissioned, agencies and other services required for this stage, with allowances for holidays, time work charge (fees), etc.

2 Special services, studies or facilities: those brought forward *and* those newly identified such as surveys, models, prototypes, structural analyses, design investigtions, material investigations, etc.

3 Special project requirements action list updated for new requirements, reviewed at project team meetings and filed with the project quality plan:

(a) Site location: access, site accommodation, utilities, ground conditions, historic records.

(b) Environment: whether it is aggressive, hazardous, extreme-temperature, wind, toxic waste, clean areas, electromagnetic radiation.

(c) Design coordination: complexity of services, restricted site, specialists not local, consultants, agencies.

(d) Security.

(e) Special requirements: high loadings, noise level, non-magnetic construction, flexibility of use.

(f) Cost in use: low energy, low maintenance, short/long life.

(g) Innovation: building type/materials not experienced by project team, need for testing, prototypes, training, investigations, need to inform client of risk.

(h) Reliability: stand-by facilities, life expectancy.

(j) Maintenance: materials with special needs, restricted access, hazard.

(k) Programming: special phasing, contract arrangements, speed of design/construction, maintaining services/operation, continuing occupancy, notify clients of consequences.

4 Completion of Stage 2.1 (outline scheme design):

(a) All studies complete as (2).

(b) Outline scheme design brochure complete.

(c) Date for client approval agreed.

(d) Outline scheme design review and action complete.

(e) Approval for submission to client with confirmation that the quality plan has been reviewed and all action required has been completed. Approval for submission to client is given by the group manager and director.

Gate to Stage 2.2 (full scheme and detail design)

1 Outline scheme design approved by the client: drawing numbers.

2 Project action list complete as (3).

3 Brief agreed and recorded: change control form and client queries list numbers.

4 General programme agreed as (1) and, if changed from Stage 2.1, recorded in terms of client change control form numbers.

5 Approval to proceed to next stage, with confirmation that all actions in Stage 2.1 are complete subject to listed provisos being completed by a given date. Approval to proceed to Stage 2.2 (full scheme and detail design) is given by group manager and director.

Stage 2.2 (full scheme and detail design)

1 Programme and resources – all as for Stage 2.1 with addition of completed drawing list under 'resources'.
2 Special services, studies or facilities identified – all as for Stage 2.1.
3 Special project requirements action list – all as for Stage 2.1 with addition of:
 (l) Special components: MOB, pre-ordering requirements, client-supplied items.
 (m) Cost plan.
 (n) Contracting strategy.

4 Completion of Stage 2.2 – all as for Stage 2.1 except the brochure and design review: refer to full scheme and detail design.
5 Approval to submit to client – all as for Stage 2.1. Approval for submission to client is given by the group manager and director.

Gate to Stage 2.3 (detail design and production drawing specification)

1 Full scheme and detail design approved by the client: drawing numbers.
2 Drawing list complete as Stage 2.2 (1).
3 Project action list complete as Stage 2.2 (2).
4 Fire Officer approved drawings received: drawing numbers.
5 Planning approval drawings received: drawing numbers.
6 Approval to proceed to next stage, with confirmation that all actions in Stage 2.2 are complete subject to listed provisos being completed by a given date. Approval to proceed to Stage 2.3 (detail design production drawing specification) is given by group manager and director.

Stage 2.3 (detail design and production drawing specification)

1 Programme and resources – all as for Stage 2.2 with the addition of:

(e)   Programme monitoring system: planned progress monitoring, linked bar chart, network, nominated operator and reporting procedure.

2   Special services or facilities identified – all as for Stage 2.2.

3   Special project requirements – all as for Stage 2.2.

4   Project documentation: the following recorded items and actions in programme:

(a)   Type of contract: confirmation with contracts officer regarding the strategy, nominated sub-contracts, preliminary works, 'spatial' contracts, etc.

(b)   Contract documentation: type and format of drawings, specifications, bills of quantities.

(c)   Document production: coding, cross referencing, interchange of information, coordination.

(d)   Provisional and prime cost sums: provisional quantities, storage of TCS items, programme advanced tendering.

(e)   PSA supplied items: TCS, MOB, Stores, SEG list.

(f)   Advanced ordering: materials in short supply, long delivery, pre-selected M and E items, proprietary products, special equipment.

(g)   Approvals required: building regulations, structural check, listed building, Royal Fine Art Commission, fire branch, utilities.

5   Completion of Stage 2.3 *may* await agreement with the selected tenderer for the production of outstanding drawings and schedules. The following must be completed before signing the contract:

(a)   Scheduled drawings completed and checked.

(b)   Specification complete.

(c)   Bills of quantities complete.

(d)   WD seminar action complete.

(e)   Project action list complete: reference numbers.

(f)   Project documentation complete as (4).

(g)   Fire Officer approved drawings received: drawing numbers.

(h)   Building Regulations approved drawings received: drawing numbers.

(j)   Certificate of completion of Stage 2.3, i.e. confirmation that all documentation is complete for construction purposes. Certification of completion of Stage 2.3 is made by group manager and director.

Gate to Stage 2.4 (construction)

1   Approval to proceed to Stage 2.4 (constructing) given subject to the detailed statement of action still to be completed during Stage 2.4.

Approval to proceed to Stage 2.4 (construction) is given by group manager and director.

Note: Here the Design Standards Office's quality plan stops because as yet there is no experience of working it in conjunction with contractors' quality plans. As the PSA Plan of Work Stages do not map exactly across to the phases of the quality management model, the mapped phase is shown in brackets after the stage heading. It should therefore be noted that the model's detail appears to be in both Stages 2.2 and 2.3, briefing would appear to be in Stage 1.0 and tendering in Stage 2.3.

The quality plan is so far not only providing a strong *internal* management framework for projects within the PSA Design Standards Office but is also beginning to supply an *external* management framework for the outside consultancies and working drawing agencies used by the PSA.

In conclusion, the PSA Design Standards Office is probably the most advanced in the UK in its application of a formal quality management system to building design and therefore being able to start applying the principles of the model to test its system for continuous improvement. It has already started to address the critical issue of feedback (perhaps the most vital element of any quality management system in effecting continuous quality improvement) through the services of a Feedback Liaison Officer operating between the Design Standards and all other PSA Design Offices and the production of project feedback brochures for selected projects that include client reaction to the finished building in operation. Very senior management is now compelled to contribute to design reviews according to the size, complexity and sensitivity of the particular project, hence ensuring chief executive commitment and support to the quality of the work of the Design Standards Office.

(From an interview with and information provided by Adrian Bell, currently Assistant Director of Army Projects Division and formerly Superintending Architect responsible for the implementation of quality management systems in the Design Standards Office – August 1989.)

Chapter 15

Case study 3: Private practice

The Building Design Practice is the largest architectural practice in the UK and has been implementing quality management procedures over the last few years. At the time of writing, all seven of its offices are shortly due to become certified to the National Quality Standard BS 5750: Part 1, 1987 under the Lloyd's Register Quality Assurance Scheme.

How does the practice/organization contribute to the building project?

The Building Design Practice provides a multi-professional design service through seventeen different professions, from architects to public works engineers through to interior designers. It also enters into joint ventures with established contractors to offer clients a design-and-build package and provides a project management service in support of its design service. It therefore contributes to the building project as a designer and, on occasions, as manager in conjunction with others.

Why is it implementing a quality management system?

It is essentially responding to client demand for the ability to demonstrate quality management capability by their professional designers and managers. With public clients such as government departments and large quasi-public bodies such as British Nuclear Fuels and Eurotunnel, it is a question of official concern that this capability can be demonstrated. In the case of the private client there is increasing interest expressed for this capability to be demonstrated, accompanying the demand for collaterial warranties, duty of care agreements and future project insurances. There is also a desire by such a large and diversely professional practice to bring together its current procedures of process control into a clearly coordinated set, and a practice-wide formal quality management system will provide this.

What difference is the system making to organizational practice?

The practice has put considerable time and effort into ensuring that the quality management system was being fully understood and successfully implemented throughout its large complement of offices, professions and individual staff. With such a large and nationally spread complement (amounting to 1200 professional, technical and administrative staff) the learning curve has inevitably been a long one, and will continue for some time to come. However, some benefits are already being perceived of the system within the practice, and these are described under the model phase inputs as follows.

People (task – skills/knowledge)
Environment (task – performance standard)

A significant outcome of implementing the system has been the definition of specific skills and knowledge of particular professional and technical staff within the practice and formalizing this information within a staff database. This means that any knowledge deficiency for a project can be easily identified so that realistic and appropriate training can be carried out. This database also provides a good basis for developing a general staff training document.

Methods (task – procedure)

Extensive controlling procedures have existed in the practice for many years, but ensuring that they are actually being used has not hitherto been possible. The introduction of the quality management system which requires the activity of auditing now informs the management whether these procedures are being used and if not, why not. A combination of different types of review for design verification is used as follows:

1   *Design sessions* are informal open discussions against a standard checklist at important points throughout the briefing, designing and specifying phases of a project.

2   *Design appraisals* are formal assessments by panels of jurors, either from within or outside the practice, as appropriate to the project, and

are limited to a number of projects at the scheme, detailing design and specifying phases.

3 *Technical reviews* are similar to design sessions and are held at the end of the detail designing and specifying phases of the project according to the degree of innovation being used.

4 *Technical checking* is the signing off by the job architect or specialist expert as necessary.

All these sessions are planned and recorded in terms of comments and corrective actions. These review procedures are all based on structured checklists and involve all levels of management in the project. Also, through the learning experience of applying the quality management system, practical methods of signing off drawings between the different disciplines are evolving in the knowledge that they will be meaningfully used.

Materials (task – information)
Facilities/equipment (task – information technology)

Improvement in information management throughout the practice is occurring and, with its nationwide spread of offices, the links to a central information database supports the rational structuring of the practice's procedures. Computer-based systems, used quite extensively by the practice, are the means by which this improved information management can be carried out.

How is the concept of the quality plan being understood and applied?

The practice's quality management system requires that each project has a job quality plan. The contents of the plan varies to suit each particular project and is formulated from a computer-based standard format comprising information on the following:

1 The client's name and address.
2 A description of the project.
3 The quality objectives in terms of:
(a) The client's brief.
(b) The services and fees agreement.
(c) The office brief to the project team.
4 The people involved.
5 The various professional procedures involved in the project.
6 The control procedures of sub-let work.
7 The project programme.
8 Review and audit reports.

9 Project administration procedures.
10 Change control procedures.

In conclusion, the practice sees its evolving quality management as the means by which its already extensively used procedures can be rationalized, structured and demonstrably carried out over its nation-wide network of offices. Clarification of roles and responsibilities, involvement of senior and experienced management in the running of projects, and the mechanisms of review and audit all give internal assurance to the practice that its design and management processes of control are practical and are therefore actually being carried out. Information management is also being given its due consideration throughout the practice and on the individual project.

(From an interview with and information provided by Harry Hosker of the Building Design Practice and the studies made by Adrian Bell in his MSc dissertation on quality management systems being applied in building design practices – October 1989.)

Chapter 16

Case study 4: Design-and-build

Kyle Stewart Limited offers a total design-and-build package to clients and has recently become certified to the National Quality Standard for its design, construction and management services. It is currently studying ways in which avaoidable costs can be identified and reduced and is being supported in this work by the UK Department of Trade and Industry and the Science and Engineering Research Council through a Teaching Company Scheme.

How does the practice/organization contribute to the building project?

Kyle Stewart Ltd offers a total design-and-build service to the client with either a negotiated cost or tender bid in response to a brief or even outline scheme design. It carries out a number of repeat-order projects for the same client, and can take on comparatively large, complex and specialized projects. It will also offer a design and management fee service as well as a design-only service and, although it generally uses its own in-house architect/environmental services/structural and interior designers, it will also use all or any of the above designers from external practices.

Therefore in its main method of contribution the organization offers the total process of the project to the client, with a single point of responsibility for both design and construction, and hence mirrors most accurately the situation for which the principles of a quality management system were devised.

Why is it implementing a quality management system?

The company's implementation of a quality management system is in response to no explicit or implicit external demand but in order to improve its own internal management processes. It is particularly keen to identify and reduce avoidable costs in its corporate and project management, and in support of this aim has embarked upon a major joint academic/industry study project entailing 8 man-years of work through the Teaching Company Scheme.

What difference is the system making to organizational practice?

The implementation of the quality management system means that, for the first time, the method by which the company works is being written down, and this has a number of benefits. These perceived benefits, which are becoming real as the implementation process develops, are described under the model phase inputs as follows.

People (task – skills/knowledge)

The documented system allows for new staff to understand the company's approach to managing projects and each department's relationship to another's during the project process. The introduction of quality improvement groups allows for the open and honest identification of problem areas in the project process that can be addressed for improvement and appropriate skills training to overcome the problems/awareness/procedures/communication.

Methods (task – procedure)
Environment (task – performance standard)

Internal audits, required by the quality management system, are a means whereby senior management can identify particular inputs into the project process so that there is a greater potential for realistic performance standards to be achieved right first time. The system is also demanding improvement in feedback and change control on projects through improved monitoring, classifying and recording the variations that occur during the project process.

Materials (task – information)
Equipment (task – information technology)

The study to identify and reduce avoidable costs is showing where communication breakdown in the transfer of information between one discipline and another (especially in the way that the information is presented) can cause errors that result in costed defects in the construction phase. Methods are being devised to demonstrate to the company departments how these defects that occur on particular projects can be traced to a combination of:

O   A lack of realistic procedures
O   A lack of quality awareness
O   A lack of education/skill training
O   A lack of communication feedback

so that the cause of these defects can be eliminated with the consequential reduction in avoidable costs. Through this approach the information and information technology input to various tasks in various phases of the project will improve with a resulting improvement in the information output of those tasks.

A further improvement envisaged from this study will be the greater utilization of the company's CAD and computer-based systems in order to improve the coordination and integration of the diverse discipline-based types of information produced by each department throughout the life of a project.

How is the concept of the quality plan being understood and applied?

Quality planning is used throughout the various phases of the project: at the initial offer stage, during the briefing phase, during the design phase where the design is being carried out in-house, and during the specifying/constructing phases in particular to identify the critical work packages to be undertaken by either the company or a specialist contractor.

The essential elements of a typical quality plan for a project (based on a master quality plan for design – pre-contract and contract for design and construction and design and management contracts) are as follows:

1   *Introduction*, which describes the purpose of the master and how it will develop into a project-specific plan.

2   *Key facts*, which describes the following specific aspects of the project:

(a)   The composition of the project team and distribution of the plan.

(b) The contact name, address, phone and fax numbers of the client's representative, quantity surveyor and consultants.

(c) The client's requirements, comprising enquiry letter, form of contract, budget cost, list of enquiry documents, design brief, drawings and submission date.

(d) The contact name, address and phone number for all statutory authorities.

(e) Dates of launch, design management, tender review and tender meetings.

(f) Presentation information in terms of architect's and engineer's drawings.

(g) Review and evaluation (see 7)).

(h) Drawing, calculation and quality checks – see (8).

(i) Design change and interface control – see (9).

(j) The dates and responsibility for the contractor's (i.e. Kyle Stewart Ltd) offer for construction proposals, specifications, design and statutory fees, offer letter, pricing information and key standards to be included in description works.

(k) Records and retention.

(l) Authorization by managing and commercial directors.

(m) Circulation table for updating.

3   *Project responsibilities* for pre-contract project director, commercial director, project design manager, project design leader/architect, project services coordinator, project engineers and architect, project pre-contract quantity surveyor, project estimate, project buyer, project planner, project temporary works engineer, construction respresentative and (following a successful offer) project director (contract) and contracts manager.

4   *Client's requirements* for submission date for tender, date of enquiry letter, form of contract and budget cost.

5   *Contractor's* (Kyle Stewart Ltd) *offer* comprising contractor's proposals (including key standards reference), specifications, design and statutory fees, offer letter including price and form of tender, and who is responsible for each.

6   *Meetings* list for launch, project design management, design coordination, tender review and tender to be held during the tender period.

7   *Review and evaluation:*

(a) For *design* with head of department technical review meetings to ensure staff are following department procedures and project design leader design coordination meetings to ensure: adequacy and interpretation of the brief; that the objectives of the brief are being fulfilled; that Kyle Stewart Ltd and the client design standards are being maintained; that any departure from cost plan is advised to project design manager; and, if there is non-conformity to the above, a project design leader report to the project design manager.

(b) For *tender review*, a meeting of all pre-contract project team representatives to assess design and commercial aspects of the total project with formal minutes if offer is successful.

(c) For *tender*, a meeting of senior management prior to the offer being submitted to agree commercial aspects.

8 *Drawings, calculation and quantity checks* depending on the complexity of project and experience of designers, detailers and other professionals and as defined in departmental procedure documents.

9 *Design change and interface control* with a 'freeze date' for when basic design parameters have been established and agreed with the client and documented; all designers obtaining additional information as necessary from the client through the project design leader; and formal project design manager design management meetings in order to:

(a) Identify where further information is required and how it will be dealt with.

(b) Highlight where pre-contract design programme is not being achieved, and determine resources to achieve target dates.

(c) Advise design team of design development since last meeting.

(d) Resolve conflicts during design development.

(e) Clarify points raised by quantity surveyor and estimators.

(f) Identify, consider and check the cost of practical alternative scheme/materials as appropriate.

(g) Arrange meetings specified in Key facts – see (2) – and project architect design coordination involving all disciplines in either drawing-board or formal meetings.

10 *Records and retentions* of all department calculations, drawings and quality-related documents until disposal as authorized by project design manager for successful offer, all archived or micro-filmed in accordance with company procedures.

In conclusion, quality improvement groups play an essential part in improving the system by getting all members of the company to carry out a long-term and systematic examination of areas of avoidable cost.

Through this approach of involving people in the identification of problem areas and determining the actions to solve them, the attitude will develop that this is 'our system for our benefit', and it is intended for continuous improvement in the company's work.

(From an interview with and information provided by John Pateman, Company Quality Director, Kyle Stewart Ltd – September 1989.)

Chapter 17

Case study 5: US practice

Skidmore, Owings and Merrill (SOM) is a leading international architectural practice that makes extensive use of computer-based systems. The USA is a country where the concept of certification to a formal national quality standard, as in the UK, does not exist. SOM now has a large office in the UK, and although it does not have a system to the exact detail described in the Quality System Standard it does have many elements of the Standard's requirements in its traditional methods of practising.

How does the practice/organization contribute to the building project?

SOM is a multi-disciplined practice with planning, structural, building services, interiors and landscaping services for the building project. On occasion, it works in conjunction with outside structural/services designers (and any other specialist designers) as appropriate to the project. It therefore contributes to the building project as a designer working in conjunction with the other project participants appointed by the client. With its US experience, it is used to working with a construction manager, as opposed to a management contractor, and expects detail shop drawings from specialist contractors.

Why is it implementing a quality management system?

This question cannot be answered directly because SOM is not implementing a formal quality management system that could be compared to the Standard. This is not to say that formality does not exist in its management of design, but rather that the practice is not working with the concept of formal quality management systems as envisaged by the Standard.

The indirect answer is that it has traditionally had a flexible but structured approach to internally project-managing the evolving design through its various stages. Elements of that approach that can be compared with the requirements of the Standard – and therefore would have the same desired effect as a formal quality management system – can be considered under the following headings.

1   *Organization*. Each project is led by a triumvirate of a senior design architect, a technical coordinating architect and a project manager, all responsible to a design and administrating director. This organizational arrangement provides for both 'people' and 'specialization' management of the design process in a project-specific manner.

2   *Review* Each project is evolved through the three phases of schematics, design development and working drawings (which includes performance specifications, detail design and production drawings for particular elements). As the design evolves through these phases, fully documented reviews are carried out for:

(a)   Code and regulation requirement analysis at the schematic design phase. This results in the development of a document used to guide the project's further development.

(b)   Client requirements by review and approval at critical points during all phases where appropriate.

(c)   Technical requirements through review throughout the design development and working drawing phases, with mock-ups as appropriate for visual and technical performance via testing of specialist elements.

3   *Feedback*. SOM's general feedback comes through their international technical committee's regular meetings and therefore direct to each project via its technical coordinating architect. Feedback is also carried out on particular projects through post-construction review sessions.

4   *Auditing*. As SOM's project management system was not as formal as that required by the Quality System Standard, the concept of auditing (which can only apply with a formal system) did not really exist within the practice.

What difference is the system making to organizational practice?

Again, this particular question cannot be directly answered as SOM's project management system is traditional in any case. However, its perceived benefits of having such a management system can be described under the model phase inputs as follows.

People (task – skills/knowledge)
Environment (task – performance standard)

New internal skills/knowledge are acquired through continuing professional development groups. Where the internal skills/knowledge do not exist, SOM draws upon those with external skills/knowledge such as meeting with district surveyors and specialist contractors during appropriate phases of the project. An understandable and structured process that is adaptable to the particular project, and was not just a rubber stamp but taken seriously, provided the right environment in which designers could perform to the best of their ability and did not militate against their creativity.

Methods (task – procedure)
Materials (task – information)
Facilities/equipment (task – information technology)

SOM's extensive use of CAD and database systems provides them with the means of:
1   Storing and retrieving the evolving design information in a structured manner through system-layering and database coordination.
2   Representing and presenting – especially through three-dimensional visualization – the design information with printouts at appropriate stage of the design's evolution for the purposes of assessment and client's review.
3   Applying automatic coding and quantification direct to the evolving design for estimating purposes.
4   Storing, retrieving, representing and presenting as-built design information for post-occupancy design evaluation and management of the finished building.
   SOM's policy regarding the use of computers in their practice is one which requires them to be used by *all* design disciplines in *all* project terms and not just by a 'computer section'. This means that the above methods and facilities provide an overall discipline in the way in which information is managed throughout the practice.

How is the concept of the quality plan being understood and applied?

A formal quality plan, as considered by a formal quality management system, is not applied by SOM's method of practice. However, a number of the elements required by such a plan do exist. Of particular significance is the approach to 'testing, inspection, examination' of the proposals of specialist contractors in response to performance specifications for particular elements, in that:

1 Physical prototypes are commissioned in order to determine visual and technical acceptance, and are produced by the specialist contractor.

2 Cost-acceptance criteria can be determined by applying value engineering techniques through a two-stage mock-up review process.

3 Reviews of the specialist contractor's shop drawings are carried out in order to meet the requirements of the architect/services/structural designer's intent.

Other elements of a project quality plan – i.e. 'specific allocation of responsibilities . . .', 'specific methods for planning, executing and verifying work . . .' – are taken into account through the practice's own internal project organization structure.

In conclusion, it can be seen that where a design practice has a well-structured internal project management approach to its work, many of the facets of a formal quality management system already exist. Such a practice – if it so desired or if the UK/European construction market started to decree that it was wise to do so – would have little difficulty in applying the principles of the model and developing a formal quality management system that could be certified against the Quality Standard ISO 9001.

(From an interview with Bob Phelan, Associate Director, Skidmore, Owings and Merrill Inc., London – August 1989.)

Chapter 18

Case study 6: European practice

With the single European market in mind, this case study examines a quality system in the wider European Community. The example selected is from Denmark, which, as well as being a member of the EC, is developing a practice that reflects the general approach of all the Nordic countries.

A particularly important feature of the application of quality management for building design in Denmark is that, unlike the UK, they have not set out with the intention of third party certification to the Standard in mind. In fact, Danish practice generally still questions the validity of the ISO Standard for the building process. The example of design practice comes from the architectural firm of Skaarup and Jespersen, Copenhagen.

How does the practice/organization contribute to the building project?

The practice provides an architectural design service which is supported by cost and time control, construction supervision and project management services for major building projects. It therefore contributes to the project as architect designer and manager with responsibility for time and cost control and construction works supervision.

Why is it implementing a quality management system?

The practice is one of the leading firms in the Danish Association of Practising Architects who, as a professional body, have initiated and developed a quality assurance and management system (QMA system).

The motivation for implementing this system in Danish architectural firms is derived from the governmental regulatory demand for such activities of all the participants in a building project, as well as the anticipation of its necessity in future major building projects in the single European market. (Their research showed that claims against architects in Denmark was a fraction of all construction liability claims and therefore the motive for implementation of a QMA system for short-term cost/benefit was not strong enough.) The essential motive is therefore that of a practice belonging to a professional body that sees the need to respond to a market demand to carry out its activities in a more formal way.

What difference is the system making to organizational practice?

The aim of the practice, in line with that of the Association, is to ensure that the implementation of any system for controlling methods of design practice recognizes the fact that the architects (who through their own personal philosophy and training come from the 'humanistic' sub-culture of Danish society) need to be motivated to use such systems in a particular way. The method chosen was to provide architects with just sufficient tools in the form of a set of manuals that deal with quality management principles related to design practice, tender documentation and contractor supervision control, and design review. Although no perceived direct benefits have been cited with regard to the practice, the generally hoped-for benefits throughout Danish architectural practices under the model phase inputs are as follows.

People (task – skills/knowledge)
Environment (task – performance standard)

Creative architect designers will be freed of bureaucracy by the appropriate and step-by-step implementation of formal working procedures.

Materials (task – information)
Equipment (task – information technology)

The creation of improved information technology systems with rational data generation and administration will improve and economize on the use of information during the design and construction management process.

Methods (task – procedure)

The formalization of work procedures helps productivity and speed in design.

How is the concept of the quality plan being understood and applied?

Although no formal quality plan is defined as described in Case Study 1, the practice uses the standard procedure of the Danish Project Phases to manage projects through the following stages.

Stages 1 and 2: client's brief and outline proposal

Here a checklist is used comprising formal questionnaires concerning the client's organization; the project and consultant organization; financial aspects and cost control; time aspects, planning and control; public authorities; the building site; functional needs and requirements, architectural and structural aspects; services requirements and needs – all to be used in meetings and discussions to ensure that the brief ultimately meets the client's requirements and needs.

Stages 3 – 5: project proposal, preliminary design, final design and tender documents

Following receipt of the client's approval of the brief, a project control procedure is implemented in the form of a stage-by stage design review comprising functional and technical cross examination (architect/engineers); cost/time updating; public authorities requirements – the results of which are recorded in internal company records and on continually updated revised drawings, specifications, calculations, cost and time schedules, etc.

Design reviews are carried out at stages 3 – 5 and are based on a review key matrix with the characteristics of 'durability', 'safety' and 'use' as headings to horizontal columns, and the influences on buildings of rainfall/moisture, temperature/sun, wind/earthquakes, live/steady loads, material fatigue/influence and sound as headings to vertical columns. The review key also contains references to production adaptation, operation and preventive maintenance, and is supplemented and completed to meet the particular project requirements. Standard forms are then completed to record the design study investigation and results for structural and architectural design at a different level of detail at each stage (e.g. checks for rainwater, ground moisture, driftsnow, condensed water, cold bridge, windtightness, corrosion, vermin, fire resistance, sturdiness, dirtiness, production appreciation, joint facing sheet/plate assembling and caulking, component connection flashing, anchoring and fastening to other components).

Stages 6 and 7: tender and project interpretation meeting

Here, following the client's approval of contractors after tender, the consultants, contractors and clients are made aware of the special problems involved in the project that require particular attention with an agenda of the client/contractors' organization during the construction period; contractors' information on works performance; contractors' comments on contract documents; consultants' information on contract drawings; and other matters.

Stages 8–10: construction, supervision and handover

During these stages a control plan is used which specifies the client's minimum requirement for quality control and assurance for the contractors' activities during construction and from which the contractor works out a quality plan on supplying and works regarding material and prefabricated production outside the site; delivery on the building site; activities during works progress; substantial completion; and handover. Also included is preparation for handover by consultants/contractors with contractors' QMA documentation according to tender documents; contractors' operation and maintenance documentation; list of works postponed/outstanding; preliminary building account; and public authorities approval/comments. All of this is formalized through the use of standard forms dealing with issues ranging from revolving schedules and procedures for progress meetings to the ascertainment of defects schedule.

In conclusion, both the practice's and Association's aims are to bring about an improvement in quality, productivity and speed in order to respond to future market competition demands for the ability to deliver results of a required quality at short notice for architectural and construction management services. In order to achieve this aim they see that the formal documented QMA system is only part – but nonetheless a vital coordinating one – of a greater whole that embraces both the application of human resource management and the greater use of information technology in architecural design practice.

(Extracted by the author from the following papers in the Proceedings of the 6th Seminar EOQC Construction Section held in Copenhagen, Denmark, 27–29 September 1989: Thygesen, T., 'Implementation of control methods and procedures within an architectural firm', pages 151–172; Hartman, M., 'Activities to motivate and educate Danish architectural firms', pages 450–459.)

Chapter 19

Case study 7: Design review

Design review is the most critical aspect of a quality management system for a building design practice. This is because the essential business and prime product output of that practice is a design, and the only way to control the process of design is by review. The nature of design is concerned with individual people reasoning about possible solutions to a building problem in conceptual terms, and the only way that activity can be externally monitored is by having the reasoning exposed at critical stages in the process. It is also important that all possible inputs to that reasoning process are known, as they will obviously influence the outcome.

The standard ISO 9004 requires that design review be carried out at the conclusion of each phase of design development by conducting 'a formal, documented, systematic and critical review' of the design results. This activity should be clearly distinguished from considering the progress of the project – which is solely related to time and cost – and is concerned with how the evolving design is meeting the previously defined requirements for grade.

The reviews, which should be carried out not only at the end of each of the main phases as described in the model but also at any intermediate point appropriate to the particular project, should 'identity and anti-cipate problem areas and inadequacies, and initiate corrective actions to ensure that the *final* design, and supporting data, meet customer [i.e. client] requirements'. In other words, review is taken to be the mechanism whereby the *evolutionary process* of design activity is conti-nually checked to ensure that requirements will be met in the final outcome.

The Standard ISO 9004 goes on to list the elements of a design review which, as appropriate to the particular phase in the design process, should contain certain items. These are divided into three categories, which, with the interpretation for a building project shown in brackets, are as follows:

A Items pertaining to customer needs and satisfaction

[These relate to the briefing/designing phases of the model and items 1–8, if carried out in full, should prevent the cause of errors that are likely to occur in those early procurement phases.]

1 Comparison of customer [client] needs expressed in the product [building] brief with (standard or innovative) technical specifications for [building] materials, products and processes.

1 Validation of the design through [building product or element] prototype tests.

3 Ability to perform under expected [building] conditions of use and environment.

4 Considerations of unintended [building] uses or misuses.

5 [Building] safety and environmental compatibility.

6 Compliance with [building] regulatory requirements, national and international standards, and [practice] corporate practices.

7 Comparisons with [other practices'] competitive [building] designs.

8 Comparison with [own practice's] similar designs, especially analysis of [own practice's] internal and [other practices'] external problem history to avoid repeating problems. [This particular item emphasizes the need for a full and rigorous feedback system, otherwise no information exists against which the comparison can be meaningfully made!]

B Items pertaining to product specification and service requirements

[These relate to the designing/specifying phases of the model and items 1–10, if carried out in full, should prevent the cause of errors that are likely to occur in these designing phases.]

1 Reliability, serviceability and maintainability [building structure, fabric and services component and element] requirements.

2 Permissible [building element assembly] tolerances and comparison with process [materials and methods of assembly] capabilities.

3 Product [whole building and elemental part] acceptance/rejection criteria.

4 Installability [buildability], ease of assembly [building element assembly], storage needs [building component replacement], shelf-life [building life-cycle] and disposability [whole building or elemental part demolition].

5   Benign failure and fail-safe [building component or element] characteristics.

6   Aesthetic [architectural] specifications and acceptance [architectural opinion] criteria.

7   Failure [building defect] modes and effects [building damage] analysis, and fault [building process deficiency] analysis. [The fundamental basis of the model provides this facility!]

8   Ability to diagnose and correct [building] problems.

9   Labelling, warnings, identification, traceability [building component or element] requirements and [building] user instructions.

10   Review of standard [building component] parts.

[This set of items emphasizes the need to fully understand the maintenance/management requirements of the future building use in the briefing phase that must logically precede the designing/specifying phases and supports the need for the critical feedback loop from the maintaining phase for a chain of conformance requirements!]

C   Items pertaining to process specification and service requirements

[These relate to the designing/specifying phases and items 1–4, if carried out in full, should prevent the cause of errors that are likely to occur in these specifying phases.]

1   Manufacturability [buildability] of the [building scheme and detail] design, including special [building material and method of assembly] process needs, mechanization [building plant], automation [building robotics] assembly and installation of [building] components.

2   Capability to inspect and test the [building scheme and detail] design including special inspection and test [building component and element] requirements.

3   Specification of [building] materials, components, including approved [building component manufacturers and specialist contractors] supplies and suppliers.

4   [Building component or element] packaging, handling, storage and shelf [building site] life, especially [building operative and completed element protection] safety factors relating to incoming and outgoing [building plant, materials and component] items.

[This set of items emphasizes the need to fully understand the construction cost and time requirements in the designing/specifying phases if time and cost targets are not to be exceeded.]

It should be possible for the reader to relate each defect cited in the following case study (which, although hypothetical, catalogues some of the typical problems that can occur in any live building project) to a deficiency in any of the phase processes. The deficiency would have been caused by not applying one or more of the element items of design review at an appropriate time. What are they? When were they not applied? What improvement is required in the practice's *corporate* management to ensure that the cause of the deficiency is eliminated?

An industrial building with offices on a difficult site

Increasing pressure for industrial and commercial development in south-east England has led to the need to build on very poor sites in difficult locations. The client has a long narrow site on a busy A road with a railway embankment to the eastern flank boundary. The site is known to have problems of unstable clay conditions, the embankment to the railway was engineered with retaining structures, and the site for the client's building has been occupied for many years by a low-rise chemical works with industrial pollutant problems. Pressure by various groups has led to the closure of the works and a planning requirement for more acceptable businesses to be established. Part of the site has also been the subject of land infill.

The client requirement is for an 'economic building' with panel and glazed curtain walling. The client is in a hurry and wants a 'fast-track' construction. He has already appointed a friend who is a curtain-wall specialist to advise him.

The client's financial adviser has suggested management contracting, and this is his request in his rambling, unstructured statement of requirements. Design, supply and install packages are required. The client, in his first interviews with the designer, shows himself, as a self-made man, to be forceful and demanding. The job has an estimated value of £25 million, and recent problems with shelved projects require the designer to improve workload and cashflow.

The designer accepts the commission and subsequently finds that there are:

1   *Defects in the foundations.* On completion of the building, movement cracking is observed in floor slabs and some internal blockwork walls.

2   *Defects in the services.* Problems are encountered with foul drainage soon after practical completion. Water is dripping through the suspended ceilings in several offices at various levels. Tenants complain of hot and cold water service problems and of the inadequate performance of the space heating system.

3 *Defects in the sound insulation.* There is growing discontent with problems associated with both external and internal intrusive noise, and flanking transmissions.

4 *Defects in the weatherproofing.* There is extensive failure with the curtain walling system, both glazed and panel, with water penetration on the west frontage and the south end walls. There is also conflict between the consultant and the trade contractor in relation to varying advice to the client.

After carrying out this exercise it will be found that the elements of design review are perfectly adequate to cope with these or any other likely situations and defects that could be considered in any imagined or real building project. This means that design review as considered by the Standard ISO 9004 suits building design, gives the level of rigour required and, with the additional application of the model, provides design practices with a means of reducing and ultimately eliminating the cause of design defects for which they are becoming increasingly liable.

It is evident from the above case study that it is the detail designing phase where the later problems in the specifying/constructing phases are generated. Therefore design reviewing in this particular phase is of critical importance.

The way in which a particular design review for the detail design of any of the structural, fabric or services elements of a building could be carried out in a practice claiming a quality management system is suggested as follows:

1 A project and product evaluation database will have been set up that is appropriate to the particular requirements of the project and relevant general design codes and standards.

2 Technical coordination with all relevant disciplines and with an emphasis specific to the project requirements will have been carried out and a specific/generic set of questions will have been formulated.

3 The project-specific requirements will have been defined in terms that can be compared with the general characteristics of the generic components and methods of assembly to be used.

4 Information will have been gathered on similar project applications from internal and external sources from feedback and fed into the evaluation databases described in (1).

5 Project-specific requirements that have been determined, agreed and approved by the client from the previous scheme design reviews will also have been fed into the evaluation databases.

6 An analysis can then be carried out that compares the detail design proposals with the project-specific requirements and general generic component and assembly characteristics in terms of:

  (a) Physical and chemical relationships and interaction between components within environments.

  (b) Aesthetic requirement satisfaction maintained from scheme design review approval.

  (c) Target cost, time and grade requirement maintained from brief review approvals.

7 Verification that the detail design requirements have been met can then be determined by the above comparison. This will be done by presenting to the client the relevant information so that if all the original time, cost and grade requirements still *cannot* be met, corrective action can be agreed and taken.

Any design practice that claims to be implementing a quality management system should be capable of demonstrating the above approach to an external second- or third-party auditor and assessor.

(From a teaching project developed with Reg Grover, Dip Arch, RIBA, Architect and Building Technology Consultant – October 1989.)

Chapter 20

Case study 8: A quality management training programme for the construction industry

The following documentation can be used as a basis for a trans-disciplinary training workshop for the main participants in a building project (i.e. the client, the designer and the contractor). The purpose of this workshop and its particular format was to ensure that the construction industry would understand the principles and application of quality management together, and consequently use quality management to help all participants work towards a common end on a building project.

This workshop was developed with the financial support of the Training Agency as a Local Collaborative Project between local academic institutions and representation from local design practices and construction companies. The format and content of the workshop are as follows.

Part I Background information based on research (Key Points to be explained at workshop)
Part II Application in practice
Park III Case study for workshop
Appendix Research findings from the Training Workshop Project

Part I   Background information based on research

Section content

A.   The philosophy of quality

B.   The mechanisms of a quality system

C.   The problems that inhibit the application of quality systems to current building practice

D.   A process model for building projects

E.   The problems of meeting the ideal model phase objectives in current building practice

F.   References

The following groups of sections can be used independently according to the quality management training need:

O   Sections A–C for basic principles and problems (this is contained in detail in Chapters 2-5 in this book)

O   Sections D–E for concept of the model (this is contained in detail in Chapter 6 in this book)

O   Section F for further background reading (this is a selection of all the references contained in this book)

The following material could be used as a basis of the teaching in the workshop. It could also be background reading before the workshop and future reference for when the workshop participants return to practice.

A   The philosophy of quality

Quality is conformance to requirements, which is attained through management for improvement by all project participants, and this should result in assurance by demonstration. Through every phase of a project there are customers who have requirements and suppliers who must conform to those requirements, but the ultimate customer is the client and the supplier is the project team.

(At this point this issue is raised for discussion concerning the role of the client as well as the designer and the contractor in terms of being a supplier and/or customer in the total project process.)

Quality management is concerned with ensuring that requirements are met first time because unless this is so, suppliers are unnecessarily increasing the cost of their processes and customers are receiving repaired products – whoever they both may be in the total project process. The four fundamentals of quality as defined by Crosby and Mortiboys are as follows:

1   The *definition* is the customer's needs and expectations. These must be translated into clearly defined and measurable requirements for building projects.

2   The *system* is prevention, which is totally ensuring that non-conformance does not occur.

3   The *performance standard* is a 100% achievement of requirements, which means that the only acceptable standard is right first time, every time.

4   The *measure* is the time spent firefighting, which is the cost of not doing things right first time.

All these four fundamentals can apply as much to the process of building projects as to the provision of any other product or service to which the principles of quality management have been successfully applied. The only factor that may inhibit their application is the divided responsibilities that exist owing to the traditional methods of procurement. However, even that problem can be overcome if all project participants are applying the principles to their own corporate management process and these are then coordinated in a particular project management process.

(At this point the issue is raised for discussion concerning the cost and responsibility aspects of methods of procurement to the four fundamentals of quality.)

Quality assurance by inspection and rejection – the conventional method of quality control in construction – cannot be superimposed onto a building project as an 'extra' with the subsequent additional cost – which is unfortunately implied in a recently published CIRIA Client Guide to Quality Assurance. This is because requirements being met first time will still not be ensured and costs will be raised – which is all in contradiction to the four fundamentals referred to above. Quality reduces cost.

(At this point the issue is raised for discussion concerning convenional practice and its relationship with an improved control process actually costing less!)

B   The mechanisms of a quality system

The four basic mechanisms of a quality management system as established in BS 5750/ISO 9000 are as follows:

1   *Organization*: requires the clear definition of the responsibilities and relationships for a total service or product.

2   *Auditing*: requires the ability to demonstrate that the tasks defined in the responsibilities are continually being carried out according to stated methods.

3 *Reviewing*: requires continuous checks on process methods and action procedures if stated requirements are not being met.

4 *Feedback*: requires the tracking of causes of errors that generate defects in measurable terms, so that processes can be improved and non-conformance to requirements can be reduced and the benefit demonstrated.

These mechanisms can be considered both as fundamental to the setting up and maintaining of a quality management system itself, and also as the additional formal actions to be carried out in the building project process; i.e. a quality system needs to be constantly reviewed, but formal reviews must be carried out from time to time throughout the building project process.

(At this point the issue is raised for discussion concerning the need for a total project system if the mechanisms are to be applied.)

The six basic elements of a quality plan as laid down in BS 5750/ISO 9000 are as follows:

1 The quality objectives to be attained.

2 The specific allocation of responsibilities and authority during the different phases of a project.

3 The specific procedures, methods and work instructions to be applied.

4 Suitable testing, inspection, examination and audit procedures at appropriate stages.

5 A method for changes and modifications in a quality plan as projects proceed.

6 Other measures necessary to meet objectives.

This means that the essential features of a corporate quality system are customized to suit a particular project.

(At this point the issue is raised for discussion concerning the quality plan concept and traditional contracts and plans of work.)

C The problems that inhibit the application of quality systems to current building practice

The factors that may inhibit these mechanisms being applied to a building project because of traditional methods of procurement are as follows:

1 Each project participant organizes his or her own particular processes according to specialism without necessarily referring to the organization of the other project participants, and consequently no overall organization for the total project ever emerges.

2   The documentation used seldom provides evidence of decision-making procedures, so tracking is impossible and auditing cannot occur.
3   Reviews – which are critical during the conceptual phases of a building project – are normally informal, sporadic and carried out against a limited subjective knowledge base rather than a comprehensive and objective one.
4   The identification of errors and their cause is discouraged because of contractual and professional liability, and consequently a positive approach to feedback cannot exist.

However, unless these mechanisms are applied to both participant corporate management and coordinated project management a quality management system cannot exist, and quality, as described above, will not be achieved.

(At this point the issue is raised for discussion concerning the degree of inhibition that exists in traditional practice and therefore how great a problem is presented.)

One of the major problems in demonstrating real benefits in applying quality management to building projects is that all methods of procurement still tend to obscure the real cost of not doing things right first time through every phase, i.e., the cost of not getting things completely right in any one phase is usually allowed for in the cost of the subsequent phase(s).

(At this point the issue is raised for discussion concerning the cost/price relationship in the different phases of the building project process.)

D   A process model for building projects

The basic framework of the model outlines six distinct phases in the life of a building project through which a chain of conformance to requirements must exist if quality is to be achieved. It is important to note that the term 'phase' does not relate entirely to the term 'stage' used in the RIBA, PSA, and BPF Plans of Work. This is because the latter term implies a sequence of periods of time which have a beginning and an end, and does not really cope with the problem of interaction over time and between stages.

The term 'phase' therefore means a particular set of tasks which, together, will achieve a stated objective and is distinct in that respect from any other phase. Therefore although any phase could recur in any stage, the application of the process model requires that every task must logically be carried out, and in the sequence defined by the phase, if the chain of conformance is to remain unbroken.

The six identified phases, all of which have distinct objectives, are as follows:

1   Briefing (including procurement)
2   Designing
3   Specifying
4   Tendering
5   Constructing
6   Maintaining (including managing)

As an example of the difference between the model phase and a plan of work stage, briefing can occur during a design, tender, construction or operating stage if there is a change in the client's requirements, or designing can occur in a construction stage if there is a change in the designer's requirements, etc. It will also logically follow from the detailed task analysis in the model that if any particular phase occurs during the life of a project, all subsequent phases must also occur and the output of any phase could feedback to the input of all or any preceding phases.

Finally, logic will demand that maintaining should comprise the continual recurrence of all preceding phases and briefing cannot occur unless maintaining has been considered in some detail in order to close the ultimate feedback loop. The phases, their objectives and their basic inputs are shown in Chapter 6.

(At this point the issue is raised for discussion concerning the relationship between traditional practice with unknown building users and the concept of closing the quality loop.)

E   The problems of meeting the ideal model phase objectives in current building practice

When the stated objectives of the six phases are compared to current building project practice it can be seen that fundamental differences occur between the ideal and reality. If quality is conformance to requirements, a clear agreement that they are reasonably achievable and objective measurement for conformance of those requirements is a prerequisite.

Observation of the practice of building design and construction in the UK shows that these three criteria are not being met in the following ways:

1   In briefing, the aesthetic requirements have to be gleaned from a wide range of subjective opinion from client to planning authority. The operating requirements are not always known as the client is not

necessarily the end user and they may change many times during the life of the building.

2   In designing, the range of possible building design solutions is infinite (even for a very well-defined brief as in architectural competitions) and judgement that any one solution is the most satisfactory is highly subjective. The long-term performance implications of detail design technology is seldom known because of continuous innovation.

3   In specifying, the division of design and construction responsibilities in the majority of UK procurement methods means that the production requirements to achieve design solutions are seldom considered in design development or agreed before construction begins. The ongoing misunderstanding between architects and builders of accuracy, tolerance and fit is an example of this.

4   In tendering, the complete production implications are never known at the general tender stage, especially with fast-track project approaches. Specialist sub-contractors usually have a very short time to consider these implications when they submit their tenders.

5   In constructing, the sub-sub-contracting nature of the construction industry makes quality control of the individual operative's work extremely difficult, and skill shortage and lowest cost targets continually force down workmanship standards.

6   In maintaining, the comprehensive operating management policy for the life of the building is seldom considered; maintenance is viewed as unacceptable, costly repair and cleaning.

Consequently, if a maintenance policy does not exist before briefing begins it will be impossible to determine whether the building in use ever conforms to the original requirements. Hence the quality loop can never be really completed and feedback will always be inconsistent and highly subjective.

All of this means that unless some fundamental changes occur in building design and construction processes, complete building project quality management cannot be successfully implemented. However, there is nothing inherent in the nature of a building project to stop these ideal objectives in each of the model phases being realized. The subsequent levels of the model propose a way of ensuring that a chain of conformance can exist throughout and between every phase of a building project.

(At this point the issue is raised for discussion concerning the fundamental changes required, both in methods of practice and in attitudes, if the ideal theory is ever to become a reality.)

F References

1 British Property Federation, *System for Building Design and Construction*, 1983
2 British Standards Institution, Code of practice for accuracy (under revision)
3 British Standards Institution, BS 5750/ISO 9000, Quality systems, 1987
4 Building Research Establishment, *Better Building means Better Building*, 1987
5 Building Research Establishment *Defect Action Sheets* (ongoing)
6 Construction Industry Research and Information Association, *A Client's Guide to Quality Assurance*, 1988
7 Cornick, T.C. *et al.*, *A Quality Management Model for Building Projects*, Department of Construction Management, University of Reading, July 1986–June 1988
8 Cornick, T.C., *Quality Management Forum Report*, Department of Construction Management, University of Reading, June 1987.
9 Cornick, T.C. *et al.*, 'A quality management model for building projects', Paper for *Quality, a Shared Commitment*, EOQC Conference, London, October 1987
10 Crosby, P., *Quality Without Tears*, McGraw-Hill, New York, 1984
11 Department of Trade and Industry, *Quality Management, a guide for chief executives* (R. Mortiboys), 1983
12 National Economic and Development Organization, *Achieving Quality on Building Sites*, 1987
13 Property Services Agency, Design Standards Office, *Quality Manual*, 1987
14 Royal Institute of British Architects, *Management Handbook* (under revision)

Part II   Application in practice

A   Plans without systems

Quality plans can be developed for coordinating projects even when the designers, contractors and subcontractors involved do not operate their own (corporate) quality systems. These project quality plans have been called quality programmes. Although they are effective up to a point, the problem is that the participants do not usually have the attitudes necessary for getting more and more of their work right first time. These attitudes are a remit of corporate quality systems where staff are part of the quality improvement process. Before the improvement process can start, however, it is necessary to establish and implement a structured approach to quality for the particular company or practice.

B   From the standard to a system

BS 5750 provides a broad model for a corporate quality system. However, it is not a simple matter of writing and discussing procedures, instruction and manuals. This does not work. People react very strongly to the imposition of written requirements for the way they work. This substantially increases the cost of implementation.

A structured approach is more cost-effective and the twelve steps to be considered when establishing and implementing a system within a company or practice are as follows:

1   Make a senior person responsible for your quality system.
2   Set up a task force and (local) working parties.
3   Agree and publish objectives, policy and action plan.
4   Create awareness in office(s) and on-site.
5   Establish organization and responsibility structures.
6   Motivate staff participation in developing and implementing the system.
7   Agree critical activities for procedural control.
8   Prepare, agree and issue job descriptions.
9   Describe your overall system in your quality manual.
10   Prepare first issue of new corporate procedures and project quality plans.
11   Implement the system and respond quickly to revision requests.
12   Audit and improve the system.

It is essential for the system to be a true reflection of the company's or practice's particular way of working. Idealistic procedures antagonize people and can stimulate a defensive (expensive) response when implementation is expected. With determined management, their commitment will be obvious with the above approach to establishing the quality system. It should be made clear that existing processes are to be defined in procedures with a view to obtaining improvements later. 'Procedures and practice (process) must be developed together.'

The quality improvement process can follow once the company or practice has a basic understanding/definition of its process. This basic definition of a company's or practice's processes is made specific for a particular project by a project quality plan.

C From the system to a plan

The corporate quality system will then provide the basic framework for a project quality plan. This should define:
1   The requirements of the project.
2   The specific allocation of responsibilities and authority during the different phases of the project.
3   The specific procedures to be applied.
4   Inspection, testing and audit programmes to verify conformance with requirements.
5   Project quality plan change control.
   Refer to Appendix A for an example for an outline project quality plan.

(At this point the issue is raised for discussion concerning how project quality plans can be encouraged – and produced – as a means of demonstrating the value of corporate quality systems in the participants' own organizations.)

D   Definitions in quality practice

1   *Accreditation Council*   The National Accreditation Council for Certification Bodies, established by authority of central government, to examine the competence of certification bodies to undertake assessment in particular fields.
2   *Certification body*   An impartial body, governmental or non-governmental, possessing the necessary competence and reliability to operate a certification system, and in which the interests of all parties concerned with the functioning of the system are represented.
3   *Quality assurance assessment*   A first- (customer), second- (firm) or third- (independent) party assessment of a firm's management capability to achieve stated objectives.

(At this point the issue is raised for discussion concerning the implications of certification of professional practices and commercial companies in the UK and the wider European and international construction market.)

Part III   Case study for workshops

A   Objectives

1   To demonstrate the results of inadequate or non-existent quality management systems within a typical construction project.
2   To examine why the situation related to the case study arose.

3   To view the consequences of an inadequate or non-existent quality management system.
4   To suggest how a recurrence of such circumstances could have been avoided.

B   Guidance

1   Study the basic elements of a quality plan (see Part II, C).
2   Study the problems described in the particular study for your level and determine:
   (a)   The management of the project.
   (b)   The management of the companies and practices (including the client) which took part in the project,
3   Establish links between the cause of errors in the case study and elements of a quality plan which, if applied, would have prevented those errors occurring in the first place.
4   State improvements required in the company's or practice's corporate management.

C   Level 1 – case study

Subject: Low-pitched roof over warehouse, office and restaurant facilities.

1   Background
This case study is concerned with the construction of a low-pitched roof over a combined despatch office and staff restaurant, which adjoins an extension to a bonded warehouse.
○   *Slide 100.* The project nearing completion. The main warehouse extension is in the foreground with a lower-level roof over the loading bay area, which adjoins the office and restaurant building under consideration.
○   *Slide 101.* This is an aerial view of the project to emphasize the nature of the work and to show clearly the lower-level building on the right.

2   Detailed information
○   *Slide 102.* The structure of the office/restaurant consists of (a) external cavity walls, (b) internal load-bearing walls, and (c) roof system sections to support profiled metal sections of roofing ('speed deck').
○   *Slide 103.* Roof system sections supported on internal skin on cavity wall and over window openings by I-section structural steel

sections onto concrete padstones. In the background is a 225 mm load-bearing brick wall, which supports the central points of the roof.

○ *Slide 104.* Close-up view of how the roof sections bear upon the internal leaf of the cavity wall. Note the rather dubious arrangement under the Building Regulations.

○ *Slide 105.* Elevation of roof system section. Note the flanges are parallel, and not tapering. The roof system section is rising from the left to right (i.e. from bearing on internal leaf of cavity wall on right to internal load-bearing wall down centre of building on left (as below)).

○ *Slide 106.* Roof system sections assembled and fitted. The RSJ running over the top of the load-bearing wall is designed to transfer the loads to the load-bearing wall below. The RSJ is clearly not resting on this load-bearing wall.

○ *Slide 107.* Emphasizes the nature of the problem : i.e. no direct bearing for the flange of the RSJ taking the roof system sections. A gap of 400 mm exists between the concrete padstone and the underside of the flange from the RSJ at the central point.

○ *Slide 108.* Similar to 107 but a different area of the roof. A smaller gap exists due to the sloping of the section.

○ *Slide 109.* The attempt at providing a quick, cheap solution to alleviate the embarrassment of the design engineer and the main contractor. (*One must ask: with what longer-term effect?*) Note the cracks from the shearing effect of placing the load on the brickwork after casting a 'make-up' concrete padstone on top of the existing incorrectly levelled padstone. Directly to the right of the padstone is a corridor. Sadly, the contractor proceeded to plaster this wall to hide the crack. An obvious error of judgement, as the stress was simply transferred to the plaster which was, in turn, to show cracking.

3 General project information

○ The project was undertaken by a large national contractor on a lump-sum basis with an incomplete bill of quantities plus drawings and specification.

○ The value of the project was approximately £3.5 million.

○ The client was a major supermarket chain requiring an increase in warehousing capacity to serve a large conurbation.

○ The contractor was asked to commence the contract at fairly short notice with only incomplete contract documents available at the commencement of site strip.

○ A civil engineering design consultant was the architect for the project.

○   The manufacturer of a proprietary roof system was nominated to supply and assemble the roof sections and associated covering, having competed with others for the work from the designer (i.e. the civil engineering consultant).

○   An order was placed by the main contractor with the roof system manufacturer as nominated suppliers.

○   Drawings were passed between all parties at all stages including final working drawings to initiate fabrication.

○   Full consultation between all parties took place at all stages.

○   Despite the apparent correctness of the working relationships involved, it was apparent that misunderstandings and misinformation had been experienced by all. This has resulted in the situation related on the slides.

4   Conclusions

○   A genuine, but avoidable, misunderstanding occurred between the three parties involved, including more than one person in each organization.

○   The misunderstandings concerned the roof and communication of the design to the construction team.

○   The construction team established all tops of load-bearing walls at the same datum. This indicated that they thought the fall in the roof would either be introduced by the covering or by a sloping section to each roof beam.

○   It was not possible to ascertain conclusively which party was at fault on conveying erroneous information, nor did it show clearly which party failed to cross-check the vital dimensions from the drawings at the working drawing stage.

○   Sadly, a poor solution was decided upon by the two principal parties (builder and designer) which will result in a defective completed building – i.e. an inherent defect to which the client is likely to have to resort to litigation, at worst, and protracted repairs, at best.

○   Had full quality management systems been in operation through each company it is doubtful that such a situation would have arisen!

Level 1 – Discussion guide

1   In what ways has this case study not met conformance to requirements?

2   What repercussions do you think that this event could have for the users of this building?

3   Is there anything else that could have been done at site level when this mistake became apparent?

4 Is there anything that someone in your position could have done to improve the situation?
5 Have you ever had anything of this nature happen to you at work?
6 How did you/do you respond to the situation?
7 Are you usually in a position where your seniors have given you a clear indication of what the customer's requirements for quality are?
8 Do they rely on you to know or ask?
9 How to you communicate these requirements to those working for you?
10 Does lack of information in your possession make this a difficult task?
11 Is there the opportunity for you to be involved in refining techniques in particular situations in the light of customer requirements?
12 Is this a task you would like to be more involved in?
13 Is there anything that you would like to see which would improve your situation in relation to the delivery of a product/service to meet customer requirements?

D Level 2 – Stages to consider in developing a quality plan

1 Identify the major contributing participants.
2 Clearly outline the nature of the relationships between them in the form of an organizational structure.
3 Draw on your previous discussion about the problems that this case has suffered from, and from your own personal experience, to highlight the issues that the plan exists to address – remember, it has purpose.
4 Divide the project into stages – briefing, designing, specifying, tendering, constructing, maintaining – and by looking at the case study analyse the ways that these tend to overlap and run into each other.
5 Explore how quality objectives could be set among the participants and discuss which party is to have an input at which stage. Consider how negotiations could most usefully be set up, how agreements could be reached and how these could be communicated.
6 Specific responsibilities then need to be allocated to implement the objectives and these responsibilities may well change throughout the course of the project. Discuss what they may be, who may hold them when and make decisions for the project concerned.
7 Explore the ways in which work instructions can be applied and decide on specific procedures.
8 Discuss and set up an auditing procedure which is capable of demonstrating that these responsibilities are being carried out as set up.

9   With the quality objectives in mind, discuss how these responsibilities might be reviewed at various stages of the project to accommodate gaps that the auditing procedure highlights or changes that need to be made. Make choices for this project.

10   Discuss how the information from this review could most constructively be fed back to participants and by whom, and set up a particular procedure for this project.

Level 2 – Issues to consider
1   What would conformance to requirements mean in this situation?
2   Has it happened? If yes, where? If no, why not?
3   What does 'right first time' mean in the context of this case study?
4   At what levels in the project does it apply?
5   What proportion of this case study involves firefighting?
6   Is this likely to continue into the use of the building?
7   Has inspection and rejection been a feature of this case study?
8   Have the nature of the relationships on this project helped or hindered the situation?
9   In what ways can you identify the impact of the relationships?
10   Has auditing taken place at any stage?
11   What review process exists?
12   Was feedback given and was it listened to?

E   Level – Procedure for case study session

1   Divide into groups of similar professions and consider the nature of the work you actually have to do.
2   On the basis of this discussion, generate a corporate quality management system suitable for your profession.
3   Discuss the case study with special reference to the problems, without considering the effects on other professions.
4   Rearrange into groups of different professions and, using the quality management systems you have developed together with the discussions about the case study, generate the quality plan for a project of this nature.

Creating a corporate quality management system – level 3
1   Need to understand the nature of your organization.
2   Need to understand the nature of your product/service.
3   Need to understand the nature of the organization's involvement in different stages of a project.

4   Explore and define the organization in terms of responsibilities for and relationships with a total service or product.
5   Consider how you can demonstrate for yourself and others that the responsibilities are continually being carried out according to stated methods.
6   How can information gained from this auditing procedure be built into a review system which, by keeping its focus on the desired outcome, means that changes to the process occur if necessary?
7   How can you organization learn from the errors it has made and from other participants on the projects you have undertaken, thus enhancing the processes of production/service delivery?

Level 3 – Issues to consider
1   What would conformance to requirements mean in this situation?
2   Has it happened? If yes, where? If no, why not?
3   What does 'right first time' mean in the context of this study?
4   At what levels in the project does it apply?
5   What proportion of this case study involves firefighting?
6   Is this likely to continue into the use of the building?
7   Has inspection and rejection been a feature of this case study?
8   Has the nature of the relationships on this project helped or hindered the situation?
9   In what ways can you identify the impact of the relationships?
10   Has auditing taken place at any stage?
11   What review process exists?
12   Was feedback given and was it listened to?

F   Services case study for use by levels 2 and 3

Subject: consequences of late addition of air conditioning.

1   Background
This case study concerns a speculative development of £1.5 million in a small London suburb. The project was started by a small firm of developers, who appointed the architects, structural and services consultants. A design was produced and a reputable firm of contractors appointed. However, before the construction work commenced, the original client ran out of money and the developers were unable to fund the building costs. They entered into partnership with a more experienced firm of developers, who were prepared to finance the completion of the development.

2   Consequences of change of client

The original developers took over the marketing while the more experienced client group assumed responsibility for finance and construction. The new clients stated that the trouble with the building was that: 'It was wrong, there wasn't air conditioning basically because it was in X-------, where there is only a small amount of parking space and it was also at the wrong end of town.'

They therefore considered, in view of these limitations on the letability of the building, that the existing building was too expensive for what was included and renegotiated the tender price. Air conditioning was added to the tender and a cheaper access flooring was specified.

3   Effect of including air conditioning

○   *Client.* The fact that the design for the air conditioning had to be completed very rapidly did not worry the client: 'They were paid a whacking great fee.'

○   *Architect.* The architect was equally dismissive: 'The first client wanted space for air conditioning installed should it ever be required – the ceiling had to be the right depth for coil fan units – then just before tender the second client decided they wanted air conditioning so the full scheme had to be done.'

○   *Services consultant.* The services consultant had a different story. First, because the development was in a mixed area where there was some residential property there could be no changes to the design that increased the height of the building. Also, they were forced to give a firm price before they had completed the design:

> 'There were a few variations associated with the air conditioning which were a result of lack of space. They couldn't make the building taller, so we had to chop the ceiling, but they didn't want it too low – it was very tight in one or two areas. The client was very keen to know the account cost. We'd given them an approximate cost but they wanted a firm price. We were pressurized to tender on the mechanical side ahead of the electrical side. One or two areas are a bit grey – which package should go in – and some got missed out.'

The services consultant was also concerned with the feelings of his staff when they were required to do a second design for the same building as he considered that 'it doesn't do them any good to see their work wasted'.

○   *The contracts manager.* By the end the contracts manager thought the job had gone quite well:

'The job benefited from a close relationship. The services going into the building were done smoothly and efficiently because [the services consultant] was involved and on hand to help.'

4 Effect of changing the access flooring

The second major area of change affecting the services concerned the access flooring. As the services consultant described it, it was 'cheap and cheerful'. The latter reported that he had experienced this floor before and strongly advised the client against using it. The criticisms were that it was not as flexible as other flooring and it squeaked. However, in addition to the finished quality of the flooring was the process of installing it in the building. The suppliers of the flooring were not prepared to guarantee the product unless they also installed it, and this proved to be a problem on-site.

o   *Services consultant.* 'The installation is a separate issue – we had no control over that. On-site the crew fixing it were appalling.' He described the floor as being fitted so badly that the electical work going in after completion of the floor was constantly having to be redone because the rough edges were catching against the wiring.

The other problem was that the electrical sub-contract was let on the basis of full-access flooring but the suppliers insisted on installing it. This meant that the floor boxes were included twice and obviously had different details and specifications. This reduced the value of the electrical sub-contract, which caused some tension on-site and also resulted in difficulties with information over details.

G Feedback questionnaire

This day's course is part of an ongoing programme of development in the construction industry to improve the understanding of quality management principles within this industry. We are intending to monitor and improve upon the effectiveness of these courses. As you are the first people to have taken part, your impressions of the day's events and any suggestions you feel to be relevant will be extremely welcome. There is no need to put your name on the form and therefore we hope you will feel able to give us completely frank answers to the questions posed. Where there is a YES/NO after the question could you circle the appropriate response and could you complete the spaces left after the other questions with your opinions.

Thank you for your time and we hope you have found the day to have been of some benefit.

1   Initially, could you give your overall response to the content of the course, commenting on anything which you feel was particularly helpful, difficult or interesting.

2   Did you consider that a day was the right length for the course? YES/NO. If not, what sort of length would you consider to be more appropriate?

3   Were you happy with having all of this on the same day? YES/NO. Would you prefer to have it broken up into different sections on different days? YES/NO. If you would have preferred a different arrangement, please indicate what.

4   Did you find it useful to have had a short introduction on quality management to read before coming to this course? YES/NO. Could the material be improved in any way?

5   Is there any other profession or member of the construction industry that you would have found it useful to talk to who was not represented in the group you attended? YES/NO. If yes, who?

6   Considering the first section on research feedback, what was the main thing that you learnt from this presentation?

7   Was there anything that could have increased the usefulness of this section? YES/NO. If yes, what?

8   Considering the second section on quality management principles, what was the main thing that you learnt from this presentation?

9   Was there anything that could have increased the usefulness of this section? YES/NO. If yes, what?

10   Considering the third section using case studies, what was the main thing that you learnt from this exercise?

11   Was there anything that could have increased the usefulness of this section? YES/NO. If yes, what?

12   Was there the right amount of time given to each of the three sections of today's course? YES/NO. If not, which were too long? Which were too short?

13   Did you consider that these sections were in the right order? YES/NO. Would any other arrangement have been an improvement? YES/NO. If yes, what?

14   If there are any other comments you have or if there is anything which you feel this form has overlooked please use the space below.

Research findings from the Training Workshop Project

1 Policy on quality training

Of the 14 companies interviewed, only one was actively pursuing the process required to be registered as a quality assured company and obtaining a BSI kite mark. This company has a Swiss parent and was of the opinion that British companies were ahead of their European partners in the field of quality assurance.

It was obvious that building service companies have a more positive attitude to quality assurance than other parts of the construction industry, probably because they are often involved in manufacturing. One such company, whose factory was quality assured, were considering registration.

Other parts of the construction industry were, on the whole, adopting a wait-and-see attitude – interested and ready to act if it became necessary to register, but not taking any active steps, such as preparing a manual for quality procedures. Companies who regularly did work for the PSA were waiting to see if they would insist on using quality-assured companies. Many people held the view that there was no point in insisting on using companies registered as quality assured unless all the companies employed on a project, including the materials suppliers, were registered.

2 Policy on training

Most companies had a training policy. Training was usually conducted in an external institution – probably reflecting the relatively small size of the companies involved in the survey. For their younger employees some form of day-release at the local technical college was usual. Otherwise, training seemed to be up to the individuals, who had to suggest to their employers what training courses they would like to attend. Several firms had short seminars or demonstrations, often held at lunchtime. The most popular subjects for these were contract law and new materials.

3 Attitude to training

Several of the more senior employees stated an interest in management training and a few were doing a masters degree in the subject. Otherwise, training seemed to consist of a few odd days during the year, for those who were lucky to have any at all. Most employees, other than those working for some kind of paper qualification, were unwilling to work at home or in their own time. This means that distance learning is unlikely to be successful and thus training which is seen as benefiting the company as much as the individual (such as that on safety or quality assurance) will have to take place in the company's time.

4 Quality assurance problems

Fourteen companies were interviewed and two or three people were asked to give their preference for training and to cite problems with quality on projects they have worked. Some of the interviewees were unwilling to discuss particular projects and discussed quality problems in general.

It should be borne in mind that the examples given were subjective – what the individuals perceived as problems. Also, there was a tendency among some to list other people's faults rather than their own. The people most likely to achieve quality are those who can see their own shortcomings and do something to rectify them. Some might say that our sample is too small, but we think that the large number of people actually interviewed from a wide range of activities within the construction industry is sufficient to show the extent of the problems with quality within the industry.

We list below our findings on quality problems. We went through the transcripts and listed all the instances of problems on quality mentioned. They were classified under various headings to give the following results. This showed that the majority of problems concern poor allocation of time and resources.

(a) Allocation of time and resources

Few companies in the survey used anything more sophisticated than hand-drawn bar charts to plan time and some were of the view that problems with time, in particular, were inevitable in the construction industry and that little could be done to improve the situation. In Japan, a country noted for its quality control, it is unthinkable to finish a project late. Resources are seen as a problem tied up with the present boom in everything and the construction industry in particular in south-east England. People are in especially short supply. One problem in this category is that not only do people not perceive it as a quality problem, but they are often unwilling to admit to a shortfall in time and resources until it is too late to do anything about it. The constraints on time were most felt by the designers in the early stages of a project caused by either the client or the designers being unwilling or unable to freeze the design at a particular point and then restricting the time for the sub-contracted designers such as structural and services engineers.

(b) Poor communications
The second largest category is poor communications, where insufficient information was supplied for someone to do the job properly, a classic being the architect who said 'you should have known about that'. This problem of communications is exacerbated by the fact that often, particularly for sub-contractors, there is no on-site supervision and site meetings may be held only once a month.

An instance which occurred on two different projects was where there were so many people involved at consultant level that it was difficult to know who was in charge and lines of communication became tangled. This proves that it is important not only to provide the correct information but also to ensure that everybody who needs to know does know.

In essence, many of the other problems appearing on this list are basically communications and at the end we shall reclassify some of these problems to illustrate this.

(c) Design errors
These were mainly omissions with a few miscalculations, all of which could be avoided. Architects failing to take account of the needs of the services was common. The really intractable design was where something new was being attempted. Only two items fell into this category. In this kind of situation it is essential for everyone concerned to be aware that new ground is being tackled.

(d) Poor workmanship
This was mainly caused by poor supervision or, in many cases the complete lack of it. Many sub-contractors employing a few people on each site find it impossible to justify a continual site presence and roving supervisors are used. In one instance even the main contractor had an office off-site. Bad workmanship on its own was rarely was a problem. Acceptable standards are handed down from the management. One agent was sacked because his idea of good workmanship was too low. In

another instance, an architect commented that there was a feeling that certain kinds of buildings (offices, for example) required higher standards of workmanship, for example, warehouses.

(e) Poor management
Most of the above category showed the result of poor supervision. The problems here are of a more general nature – organization of who does what and when on-site (e.g. who cleans up before finishes are put on).

(f) Technical problems with materials
The largest group in this category are goods arriving on-site not matching the specification that was ordered – poor quality bricks or tiles; air-conditioning equipment which did not meet specification. Poor handling of materials was another problem, with the most difficult problems being those of handling materials new to the industry.

(g) Poor specifications
These are inadequate specifications by architect or quantity surveyor – or one specifying one item and the other something different. Contractors sometimes ignore specifications and order something else – with adverse results.

(h) Site conditions
All these instances were of public authorities failing to do surveys of land or buildings before commencing and then discovering that there were unforeseen problems.

(i) Inexperienced staff
Unsupervised inexperienced staff caused a few problems. One more senior person commented that where clients negotiate lower fees, they should not be surprised if they have inexperienced staff on-site with a consequent propensity for mistakes to occur.

(j) Contractual
These problems occur when different forms of contract are used. For example, a client changed from nominated to domestic sub-contractors and yet still thought that he had the right to deal with them directly.

(k) Buildability
Buildability problems arise where a contractor is not on hand at the design stage to advise on easier or more economical methods of construction.

(l) Inadequate training
Only one comment related to inadequate training, and this was a general one. It would appear that inadequate training is often a scapegoat for poor communications or management.

Classification under the above headings was rationalized under fewer headings, as many of the factors could be listed under communications in its broadest sense – inadequate specification, poor management, buildability and even inadequate training. Some could be reclassified as poor allocation of time and resources. Only very few fitted into neither category. This was illustrated in a pie chart which showed that about two thirds of the problems are caused by inadequate communications; over one quarter by poor allocation of time and resources and less than 10% by fairly intractable problems, such as new forms of design or new materials or poor quality of materials supplied.

References

1 Mortiboys, R., *Quality Management, A guide for chief executives*, Department of Trade and Industry, 1983
2 Power, R.D., *Quality Assurance in Civil Engineering*, Construction Industry Research and Information Association Report No. 109, 1985
3 Ibstock Building Products Ltd, *Quality Management Commitment*, 1987
4 Bovis Construction Ltd, *Quality Management System*, 1987
5 British Standards Institution, BS 5750 Series/ISO 9001-9004, 1987
6 Property Services Agency, *Quality Assurance Publication*, Directorate General of Design Services, 1986
7 Property Services Agency, Design Standards Office, *Quality Management System Manual*, 2nd edition, 1988
8 Denny, R., *The British Property Federation System for Building Design and Construction*, 1983
9 Brandon, G., *A Client's Guide to Quality Assurance in Construction*, Construction Industry Research and Information Association Special Publication, 1988
10 Royal Institute of British Architects, *Quality Assessment Scheme, Model for a Quality System Manual*, 1990
11 *Quality Assurance*, Guidelines to Registration of Quality Systems to BS 5750 for Architectural Practices, Yarsley Quality Assured Firms Ltd, 1988
12 Lush, D., Technical Director of Ove Arup Partnership, 'BS 5750 unnecessary says engineering firm', *Building Today Journal*, 31 August 1989
13 *The Manual of Professional Practice for Quality in the Constructed Project*, American Society of Civil Engineers, 1988

14 *Building Britain 2001 Report*, Centre for Strategic Studies in Construction, University of Reading, 1988

15 *Achieving Quality on Building Sites*, National Economic and Development Office, 1987

16 Cornick, T. and Gill, M., *A Quality Management Training Programme for the Construction Industry*, Training Agency Local Collaborative Project, 1988

17 Atkins, W.S., *Latent Defects in Building, an Analysis of Insurance Possibilities*, National Economic Development Office, 1985

18 *Build – Building User's Insurance Against Latent Defects Report*, National Economic Development Office, 1988

19 Goodacre, P., Cornick, T. and Kelly, J., *Cost Factors of Dimensional Coordination*, Final Report, Science and Engineering Council Research Project, University of Reading, 1979

20 Cornick, T. and Pateman, J., *Programme to Identify and Reduce Non-Conformance Costs*, Science and Engineering Research Council/ Department of Trade and Industry Teaching Company Scheme, Kyle Stewart Ltd and University of Reading, 1988-1991

21 Gray, G. and Flanagan, R., *The Changing Role of Specialist and Trade Contractor*, Chartered Institute of Building, 1989

22 Broadbent, G., *Design in Architecture*, John Wiley, Chichester, 1973

23 Powell, J., Inaugural Professorial Lecture, School of Architecture, Portsmouth, 1988

24 Mackinder, M., *Studies in Information Usage in Architectural Practices*, Institute of Advanced Architectural Studies, University of York, 1985-1987

25 Cornick, T., *Construction Management Forum Interim Report*, Department of Construction Management, University of Reading, 1989

26 Cornick, T., 'A quality management model for building projects', *International Journal of Project Management*, **6**, No.4, November 1988

27 IBM United Kingdom Ltd, *Quality Improvement Mission*, 1986-1988

28 Cornick, T. and Wix, J., *Information Management for the Construction Industry*, National Economic and Development Office, 1990

29 Crosby, P., *Quality without Tears*, McGraw-Hill, New York, 1984

30 Cornick, T., *Quality Management Forum Report*, 1987

31 Lawson, B., *How Designers Think*, Butterworth Architecture, London, 1983

32 Cornick, T., Broomfield, J., Grover, R. and Biggs, W.D., *A Quality Management Model for Building Projects*, Science and Engineering Research Council Project, University of Reading, 1986-1988

33 Royal Institute of British Architects Management Handbook, *Plan of Work* (currently under revision)

34 Royal Institute of British Architects, *Quality Assessment Scheme Proposal*, 1989

35 *Dataease, Version 2.5*, Release 2 Software Solutions Inc., USA, 1986

36 *'Dry Envelope' Concept*, Conder Group plc, 1987

37 Murray, J., *A Model for Guiding Clients and the Design Team during Briefing*, University of Reading, 1988-1990

38 Riley, J., *Better Briefing Means Better Building*, Building Research Establishment, 1987

39 Construction Management Forum, *Final Report*, Centre for Strategic Studies in Construction, University of Reading, 1990

40 Brandenburger, J., Project Client Consultants, UK, 1989

41 Paterson, J., *Information Methods for Design and Construction*, John Wiley, Chichester, 1977

42 Paterson, J., *Architecture and the Microprocessor*, John Wiley, Chichester, 1980

43 Ching, F.D., *Architecture: Form, Space and Order*, Van Nostrand Reinhold, New York, 1979

44 Cruickshank, D. and Wyld, P., *London: the Art of Georgian Building*, Butterworth Architecture, London, 1977

45 Atkin, B. (ed.), *Intelligent Buildings*, John Wiley, New York, 1988

46 Ransom, W.H., *Building Failures: Diagnosis and Avoidance*, E & F Spon, London, 1981

47 Allen, W., 'Failures are good opportunities for learning', Keynote Paper presented at the International Council for Building Research, Studies and Documentation, Advancing Building Technology Congress, Washington, DC, 1986

48 Rich P., *Principles of Element Design*, 2nd edition, George Godwin, London, 1982

49 Property Services Agency, *Method of Building: Technical Guidance on Windows*, Fifth Programme, 1987-1990

50 Powell, M. (ed.), *Buildability: an Assessment*, Construction Industry Research and Information Association Special Publication, 1983

51 British Standards Institution, BS 5606: Code of accuracy (under revision)

52 *Coordinated Project Information for Building Works*, Coordinating Committee, 1987

53 *Standard Method of Measurement of Building Works*, 7th edition, Royal Institute of Chartered Surveyors, The Building Employers Confederation, 1988

54 Haverstock Associates, *Quality Management System Manual*, 1989

55 *Faster Building for Commerce Report*, National Economic and Development Office, 1988

Index